# THE POWER IN CUBASE

# THE POWER IN CUBASE

## Tracking Audio, MIDI, and Virtual Instruments

Matthew Loel T. Hepworth

Hal Leonard Books
An Imprint of Hal Leonard Corporation

Published in 2012 by Hal Leonard Books
An Imprint of Hal Leonard Corporation
7777 West Bluemound Road
Milwaukee, WI 53213

Trade Book Division Editorial Offices
33 Plymouth St., Montclair, NJ 07042


Printed in the United States of America

Book design by Adam Fulrath
Book composition by Kristina Rolander

Library of Congress Cataloging-in-Publication Data

Hepworth, Matthew Loel T.
 The power in Cubase : tracking audio, MIDI, and virtual instruments / Matt Loel T. Hepworth.
    p. cm.
 Includes index.
 ISBN 978-1-4584-1366-6
 1. Cubase. 2. Digital audio editors.  I. Title.
 ML74.4.C8H46 2012
 781.3'4536--dc23
                              2012017846

ISBN 978-1-4584-1366-6

www.halleonardbooks.com

# Contents

## Chapter 1

## Chapter 2

## Chapter 3

## Chapter 4

## Chapter 5

## Chapter 8

# PREFACE

## Dreaming of Digital

Let me take you back to February of 1984. Once strictly reserved for classical music, audio CDs of pop music were just hitting the record-store shelves. As a fan of Peter Gabriel, I was thrilled to repurchase the CD version of his fourth album, known in the United States as *Security*. (For those of you in the know: yes, it is a West German "Target" disc.) As I stood at the checkout counter holding the shrink-wrapped package in my hands, I noticed a small, pink band on the cover artwork that read, "Full Digital Recording." This was the first time I'd ever seen such a listing. It meant the music was digitized into a series of numbers, and only when the consumer played the CD was it reconstructed into an analog signal. I couldn't fully grasp the concept, but it piqued my interest in recording music digitally.

It wasn't until I got home and listened to the CD (CD players didn't appear in cars until late 1984) that I started to understand the advantages of digital. First and foremost, there was no tape hiss. Since the multitrack recording was done with a digital recorder, there were none of the ubiquitous tape artifacts that we'd all put up with for so long. Next, my amplifier and speakers were challenged by the upper limits of the dynamic range. Yet the quiet passages revealed subtleties once reserved only for those who could afford the most esoteric and expensive of phonographs. I thought to myself, "Someday I'll be able to make my own digital recordings."

## "Someday" Only Took Eight Years

Throughout most of the '80s and '90s, I worked in music stores selling keyboards and recording equipment. It was a great way to learn about the newest digital technology, and it left my nights free to play gigs. In 1992, we received our first shipments of a new product from Alesis known as the ADAT (Alesis Digital Audio Tape). It was the world's first affordable digital 8-track recorder. Suddenly, for just under $4,000, musicians and engineers alike could own a digital multitrack recording device. To say that it revolutionized the project and home-studio market would be an understatement.

While it was the first and therefore most affordable digital multitrack recorder on the market, I still needed a mixer, compressors, effect processors, and a 2-track DAT machine to mix to. I also needed boxes of cables and S-VHS tape stock with which to feed the ADATs. While the ADAT made the dream of the digital home-recording studio a reality, it was still an expensive proposition.

## The Dawn of the DAW

Music software had been around ever since the early '80s. In fact, I still have the music cartridges that in 1982 allowed me to sequence music on my Commodore 64 even before there was MIDI. (I still use my Commodore 64 computers with the MSSIAH MIDI cartridge from 8bitventures.com.) But in 1993, Steinberg released Cubase Audio. It allowed Atari Falcon (computer) owners to run Cubase MIDI tracks and up to eight digital audio tracks simultaneously. I had been using Steinberg Pro16 MIDI sequencing software on my Commodore 64 for years, but I didn't get into Cubase Audio until it became available on Windows in 1996. Together with my Yamaha CBX-D5 and CBX-D3 audio interfaces, I could play back just as many tracks as my 8-track ADAT.

### Time Becomes Nonlinear

Cubase Audio also allowed me to use the same digital editing techniques I'd been using on MIDI tracks for years. Suddenly I could cut, copy, and paste audio data from within the Cubase timeline. This kind of editing was unheard of on the ADAT because of its tape-based format, which rendered its timeline linear. Not only did Cubase Audio allow me to move audio data around the timeline as easily as I could with MIDI data, it also did it nondestructively. In other words, all of the original versions of my Audio tracks were retained on the hard drive. The price of this computer-based system was even less than the ADAT technology.

### The Real World Becomes Virtual with VST

Later in 1996, Steinberg created VST, or Virtual Studio Technology. VST created virtual signal processors (such as EQ, compressors, chorus, and reverb effects) right inside of the computer. My gigantic mixer and racks of external signal processors were quickly becoming obsolete. Within a few years, Steinberg added VSTi, or VST Instruments, to Cubase, which created virtual synthesizers, samplers, and drum machines inside of the computer. At that point, my synthesizers and samplers were getting obsolete too. Fortunately, this was also when eBay hit the scene, and I used it to sell off my hardware.

### Cubase Is a Complete Recording Studio

Fast-forward to present day, and Cubase has become an entire recording studio right inside of your computer. Sure you'll still need mics, MIDI and audio interfaces, a few cables, instruments, speakers, and inspiration to make it all happen. But never before has the recording studio been more accessible to musicians and music enthusiasts alike. Consider this: Cubase LE and AI (limited editions of Cubase that ship with many third-party hardware products, Steinberg products, and Yamaha products) provide sixty-four audio tracks. That's sixty more tracks than the Beatles ever had! We really do live in exciting times.

### Be Careful What You Wish For

Now that you have an entire recording studio in your computer, learning how to use all of it can be a daunting task. Imagine you just walked into a state-of-the-art commercial recording facility and noticed all the buttons, switches, knobs, cables, and hardware that filled the control room. Now imagine you have to sit in the "big chair" and take charge of a recording session. Are you ready to do that? My guess is that you'd be besieged by the prospect of being thrown into the role of engineer and running all of that gear.

Well, by purchasing Cubase and running it on your computer, you are sitting in the big chair. I've had the advantage of gradually experiencing the digital revolution throughout its various stages. But if in 1984 I'd been thrown into a recording studio and told to record music, I'd be completely overwhelmed and intimidated. I imagine that's how many of you feel right now. It might even be the reason you are reading this book.

## How to Use This Book

I have faith that you will be able to become an accomplished Cubase user and do things I could only dream of doing back in 1984. But to do so, I recommend that you learn Cubase as you would a new musical instrument. Many of you play some sort of musical instrument. Unless you are a prodigy, wrangling the first notes out of the instrument didn't meet world-class standards. However, through daily practice and learning from mistakes, you became a competent musician. Or at the very least, you've learned enough to allow the instrument and the music you make with it to enrich your life.

If you apply that same approach to learning Cubase, you will be able to record your music (or the music of others) on your computer in the comfort of your home, project studio, or commercial facility. To say that Cubase and digital music production have irrevocably augmented my musical experience, as well as provided me with countless positive experiences, would be an understatement. I truly want you to have similar experiences with Cubase. It can happen for you if you practice each day, take breaks when overwhelmed, learn from your mistakes, and revel in your accomplishments. The music you make can enrich not only your life but also the lives of others. It can provide you with an outlet and a living, and it has the potential to change the world. When all is said and done, it will leave a legacy of your time on Earth. Music has that power. But like so many other of life's experiences, it is better when shared with others.

With all that in mind, roll up your sleeves, take a deep breath, and open your mind and heart to the opportunities the digital age has to offer you.

# ACKNOWLEDGMENTS

I'd like to thank Karl Steinberg and Manfred Rürup for having the vision and courage to create such revolutionary products.

Thanks to Bill Gibson and everyone at Hal Leonard for bringing me into this project. Thanks also to copy editor Joanna Dalin Sexton for making the book readable. Together, they all made it a joy to create this book and bring the information to you.

Thanks to Alan Macpherson, Brian McGovern, and Greg Ondo at Steinberg North America, and Melanie Becker at Steinberg Media Technologies GmbH. Every author should be lucky enough to have the support of such wonderful people.

Speaking of wonderful people, thanks to my sister Jillian S. Clark for being my champion and best friend, and to my dad, the late Dr. Loel T. Hepworth, for recognizing the autodidact in me and providing me with an environment in which I could flourish.

This book is dedicated my mother, Connie Jo M. Hepworth-Woolston. In the classroom, onstage, and in real life, her exquisite grace and profound passion continue to inspire many to live and love without limits. Thank you for everything you do for me, especially helping me to hear and see the music in dance and motion.

# Chapter 1
# Setup, Installation, and Configuration

If you've purchased this book, I will assume that you have a computer and have purchased a copy of Cubase 6, Cubase Artist 6, or Cubase Elements 6 (herein, all will be referred to as Cubase). That's great, but there are other items that are required to take full advantage of what Cubase has to offer. Then, when you have all of those items, you'll need to know how to hook them all up and how to configure your computer to get your components working properly. In this first chapter, you will learn about:

- How to use this book with your level of Cubase.
- Minimum system requirements for Cubase.
- Running Cubase in 32-bit or 64-bit mode.
- Installing Cubase on your computer.
- Using the eLicenser Control Center and USB-eLicenser.
- The importance and process of creating a MySteinberg account.
- The differences between Cubase on Mac OS X and Windows.

## Using This Book with Different Levels of Cubase

For several years now, Steinberg (the company that creates Cubase) has used the "good, better, best" approach to making different levels of Cubase. You'll notice I said "levels," not "versions." That was on purpose. You see, the version of software usually denotes how up to date an application is; the higher the version number, the more current the software. However, software also comes in different levels that offer a "features versus price" balance. For example, with the release of Cubase 6, there are three levels: Cubase 6 Elements, Cubase 6 Artist, and the fully featured Cubase 6. Each level has different features for a different cost. While you can use this book with any level of Cubase, it was written with the full Cubase 6 level in mind. That is to say, I'll be covering features and operations in Cubase that may not exist in Cubase Artist or Cubase Elements.

However, one of the most magical advantages of software is how easily it can be upgraded. Not only can you upgrade to a new version at a reduced cost (from Cubase 5 to Cubase 6), but you can also upgrade from a lower level to a higher one (from Cubase 6 Artist to Cubase 6). If you have either the Elements or Artist level of Cubase, and you find a feature of Cubase that would enhance your productivity, you can simply upgrade to a higher, more fully featured level. Steinberg offers those upgrades at http://www.steinberg.net. You can also find a feature-by-feature comparison of all the Cubase levels on their website.

So please bear in mind that I won't be indicating what features come in which level of Cubase. It would behoove you visit the Steinberg website and familiarize yourself with the features of your level of Cubase. That way, you won't spend time learning about features your level doesn't currently have.

# Does Cubase Run Better on a Mac or PC?

Thirty years after the birth of MS-DOS (Microsoft Disk Operating System) and twenty-seven years after the birth of the Macintosh, the debate over which platform is better rages on. Fortunately, Cubase is cross-platform; it runs on both Mac OS X and Microsoft Windows. Both the Mac and Windows versions are included on the installation DVD. In fact, there are only miniscule differences between the operation of Cubase from one platform to the other. So miniscule, in fact, that many users (me included) have to remind themselves which platform they're currently using. For the most part, it really comes down to what *you* like better or what type of computer you currently use. With Cubase, you have freedom of choice.

However, sometimes that decision is made for us when we find a VST plug-in (either a virtual instrument or effect) that only runs on one platform. The vast majority of plug-ins are cross-platform. But I occasionally find an indispensible or exciting plug-in that only runs on Mac OS X or Microsoft Windows. If I want to avail myself of using that plug-in, I'd better use the platform upon which it runs.

I've used the following criteria to help my clients choose a platform: find the application (program) you want to use, determine which platform it runs on, and then find out if any third-party plug-ins you want to use are available on that platform. By using those criteria, you will quickly determine whether a Mac or Windows PC will better serve your computing needs. If you're like me and already own an Intel-based Mac, you can always use Apple's free Boot Camp software (which is included in Mac OS X) to allow your Mac to boot, and run Cubase 6 with Microsoft Windows. All it takes is buying a copy of Windows. I've used Boot Camp for years, and I can verify it's a very reliable method of running Windows on a Mac.

# Recommended Minimum System Requirements

Many new users will ask the question, "How modern and powerful does my computer need to be to run Cubase?" Steinberg has listed their minimum system requirements on their website. It's a good idea to take a look and see if your computer meets that minimum requirement.

I will list Steinberg's requirements here so that I can explain why they're important. But first, I'll define what each of these items are.

## Operating System

This is the software that makes the computer functional. Every computer (with very few exceptions) will come with an operating system (herein referred to as "OS") preinstalled. Macs will come with some version of OS X, while PCs will come with some version of Windows. As long as you've had your Mac- or Windows-compatible PC computer for a year or two, it will probably have a compatible OS.

## CPU

This is an acronym for Central Processing Unit. You can think of the CPU as the "brain" of your computer. Many of today's modern CPUs are a multicore design. It does all the calculations and number crunching that allows Cubase to turn your computer into a recording studio. Each core is a CPU, so a multicore CPU is a "sandwich" of two or more CPU cores.

## RAM Memory

This is the "workspace" into which the OS loads applications and documents. It's ultrafast, and you can never have too much RAM. (See "Deciding to Run Cubase in 32-Bit or 64-Bit Mode," later in this chapter.)

## Hard Disk Space

This is where the OS, applications, and documents are stored for later recall. DAW (Digital Audio Workstation) applications such as Cubase will require more hard disk space to carry out their primary function, which is making music. As with RAM memory, you can never have too much hard disk space.

## Display Resolution

This is how many rows of pixels (dots on a computer screen) your monitor can display. There are horizontal and vertical measurements. My personal favorite is a resolution of 1920 x 1200 (1920 rows across by 1200 rows top to bottom.) The higher the resolution, the more "stuff" you'll be able to see on the display. Conversely, low resolutions can make it impossible to see the Cubase user interface in its entirety.

## Audio Interface

While all computers will come with some sort of sound device, these are woefully inadequate for music production. Therefore, a high-performance audio interface is recommended. The audio interface is used to get sound into and out of your computer and Cubase. (See "Choosing an Audio Interface," chapter 2.) Most, but not all, audio interfaces come with CoreAudio (Mac) or ASIO (PC, Audio Streaming Input-Output) drivers, or use a generic driver from within the OS.

## DVD Dual-Layer Optical Drive

Cubase comes on a dual-layer DVD and therefore can only be installed from a compatible DVD drive. If your computer is a netbook or a MacBook Air, which do not have onboard DVD drives, you'll need to attach an external (USB or FireWire) DVD drive to install Cubase. Alternately, you can use a DVD drive–equipped computer to create an ISO image of the DVD, copy that image to a flash drive or other USB storage device, then connect that device to the computer upon which you wish to install Cubase.

## USB Port

Universal Serial Bus, or USB, ports are ubiquitous on all modern computers. Cubase uses a copy-protection device called the USB-eLicenser that must be connected to the computer's USB port before Cubase will launch.

## Internet Connection

Once you have Cubase installed, you'll need to activate the product via the Internet. I would also strongly advise you to register your copy of Cubase at http://www.steinberg.net. Registration requires that you create a MySteinberg account and is highly recommended for a number of reasons, not the least of which is getting your USB-eLicenser replaced should it ever become damaged or lost.

Now that you know what all of these specifications are, here are the basic minimum system requirements for both platforms that Cubase runs on:

### Mac
- Mac OS X version 10.6 (Snow Leopard) or higher (10.7 [Lion] compatible).
- A dual-core CPU or higher (for example, an Intel Core 2 Duo or higher).
- 2 GB (gigabytes) of RAM memory.
- 500 GB (0.5 terabyte) hard disk.
- Display (computer monitor) capable of 1280 X 800 or higher.
- CoreAudio-compatible audio interface.
- DVD-ROM dual-layer–compatible drive for installation; CD-R or DVD+/-R for audio CD burning or archiving.
- One open USB port for USB-eLicenser.
- Internet connection required for product activation.

### PC
- Windows 7 32-bit or 64-bit.
- A dual-core CPU or higher (for example, a dual-core AMD, Intel Core 2 Duo CPU or higher).
- 2 GB (gigabytes) of RAM memory.
- 500 GB (0.5 terabyte) hard disk.
- Display (computer monitor) capable of 1280 X 800 or higher.
- Windows-compatible audio interface, but ASIO compatibility highly recommended.
- DVD-ROM dual-layer–compatible drive for installation; CD-R or DVD+/-R for audio CD burning or archiving.
- One open USB port for USB-eLicenser.
- Internet connection required for product activation.

# Deciding to Run Cubase in 32-Bit or 64-Bit Mode

Before we can install Cubase, we'll need to know about the memory-addressing modes of 32-bit and 64-bit. Cubase can run in either mode. The mode you choose will have nothing to do with the *sound* of Cubase but rather how much memory it can use. Simply put, the amount of RAM memory a computer and/or application (such as Cubase) can address is determined by three things:
- The amount of RAM installed in the computer.
- The 32-bit or 64-bit architecture of the OS.
- The 32-bit or 64-bit architecture of the application.

Are you confused yet? Well, you're not alone. You see, for a long time, RAM memory was exorbitantly expensive. (I remember, back in 1987, paying $584 for 16 MB [yes, megabytes] of RAM!) Therefore, computers didn't come with much, and OSs and applications were small enough that they didn't require much. But today, 2 GB of RAM is barely enough to load your OS, let alone run high-performance recording software such as Cubase. Having an abundant amount of RAM is critical, but only if your OS and applications can utilize, or "see," your computer's installed RAM in its entirety.

To illustrate this as simply as possible, let's use the example of a computer with 3 GB of RAM. In this scenario, using a 64-bit OS or application would be of *no* benefit. That's because a 32-bit architecture can only utilize 3 (or sometimes 3.5 to 4) GB of RAM. However, if the computer had 4 or 8 GB of RAM or more, then using both a 64-bit OS and application would have distinct advantages: the user would be able to load more applications and load more data into those applications, and the OS wouldn't be using the page file as much. (Paging occurs when the amount of physical RAM memory becomes too low during the course of performing tasks on a computer. In that case, the OS must offload some of that data back onto the hard disk to clear some RAM space in which to work. The paging process can seriously impede your workflow, because the hard disk is about one thousand times slower than the RAM.)

## 32-Bit or 64-Bit Mode for Mac Users

Making the decision to run in 32-bit or 64-bit mode is simpler for Mac users. First, since Cubase 6 requires that you use OS X 10.6 (Snow Leopard) or 10.7 (Lion), your OS is already 64-bit compatible. Plus, unlike the Windows version, Cubase for Mac installs in both 32-bit and 64-bit versions. (See "Enabling 64-Bit Mode on a Mac" later in this chapter.)

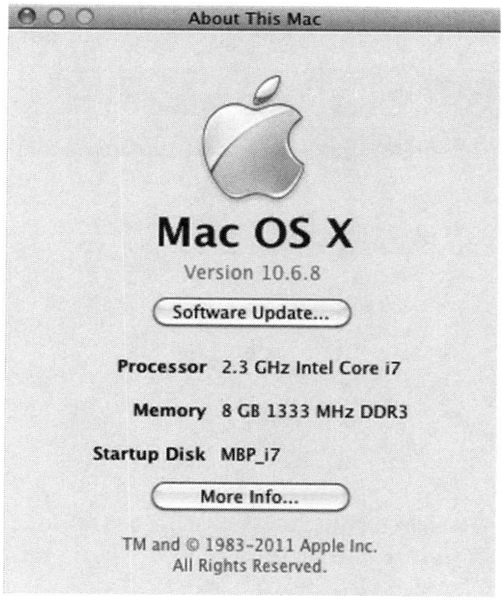

Figure 1.1: The About This Mac display

Next, you'll need to determine how much RAM your Mac has. Click on the Apple (logo) menu in the upper left-hand corner of your display, and select About This Mac.

Chances are very good that the OS version will be 10.6.X or 10.7.X. So what you really want to determine is the amount of installed RAM memory. In Figure 1.1, you can see that this Mac has 8 GB of RAM. Therefore, it would be beneficial to run Cubase in 64-bit mode.

But before I show you how, there are some extenuating circumstances that may require you to keep Cubase in its default 32-bit mode:

### 32-Bit Only Features
As I write this book, there are still a handful of features and operations that cannot be performed while running in 64-bit mode. For example, score printing and ReWire can only be used while in 32-bit mode. (Current information regarding 64-bit compatibility can be found at www.steinberg.net.)

### Plug-in Compatibility
Some 32-bit plug-ins simply cannot work in 64-bit mode. Steinberg uses a technology called the VST Bridge to maintain 32-bit compatibility of plug-ins even when running Cubase in 64-bit mode. However, my experience has been that not all third-party plug-ins behave properly in 64-bit mode.

As time marches on, the list of operations dependent upon 32-bit or 64-bit mode will diminish. The third-party plug-in developers have and will offer updates to their software that add 64-bit architecture, thereby bypassing the need for VST Bridge. But for now, you will need to do a little research to deduce which mode is better for you.

## 32-Bit or 64-Bit Mode for Windows PC Users
Determining which mode to install and use on a Windows PC is a little more challenging. First of all, you'll need to determine if your version of Windows is 32-bit or 64-bit. Second, you must know how much RAM your PC has. Fortunately, those are easy tasks. Click on your Start button in the lower right-hand corner of your display, then click on Computer. In the window that appears, click on System Properties in the Taskbar.

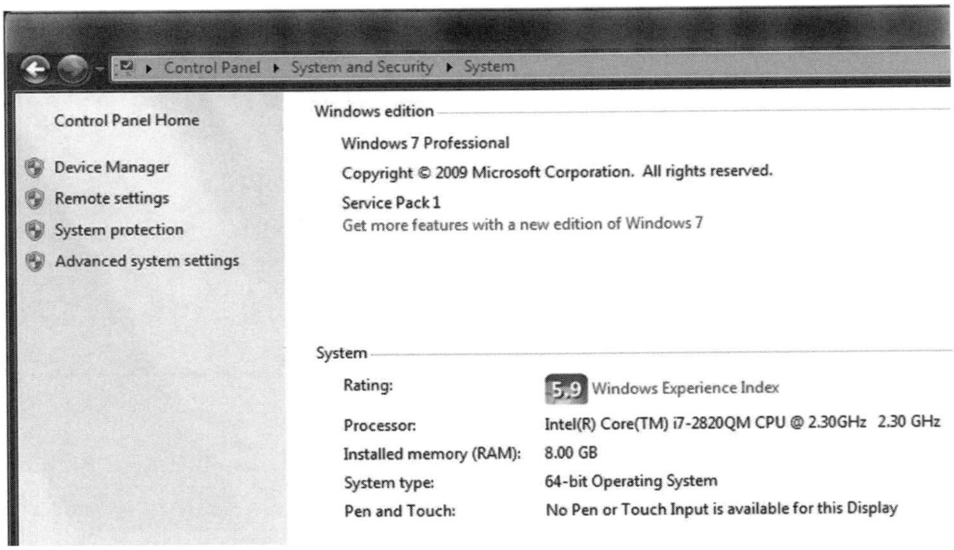

Figure 1.2: The System Properties window

If the OS architecture is 64-bit, then you can install Cubase as a 64-bit application. However, if the installed RAM is 4 GB or lower, then the benefits of 64-bit will be limited. Only if your computer has more than 4 GB of RAM can you fully realize the benefits of using 64-bit mode.

When it comes to installing Cubase for Windows, you can choose either the 32 or 64-bit version. However, I strongly recommend that you install *both* versions. Yes, it will take a very small amount of hard disk space to do so. However, as with the Mac platform, there are some circumstances that must be considered:

### 32-Bit-Only Features

As I write this book, there are still a handful of features and operations that cannot be performed while running in 64-bit mode. For example, score printing and Rewire can only be used while in 32-bit mode. (Current information regarding 64-bit compatibility can be found at www.steinberg.net.)

### Plug-In Compatibility

Some 32-bit plug-ins simply cannot work in 64-bit mode. Steinberg uses a technology called the VST Bridge to maintain 32-bit compatibility of plug-ins even when running Cubase in 64-bit mode. However, my experience has been that not all third-party plug-ins behave properly in 64-bit mode.

That's why I would recommend installing both versions. That way, you can switch between 32-bit and 64-bit modes simply by launching the appropriate version. For example, if you need to print a score, just launch the 32-bit version. When you need to load a big project that requires more RAM, launch the 64-bit version. You can run the 32-bit mode of Cubase even if your version of Windows is 64-bit.

As time marches on, the list of operations dependent upon 32-bit or 64-bit mode will diminish. The third-party plug-in developers have and will offer updates to their software that adds 64-bit architecture, thereby bypassing the need for VST Bridge. But for now, you will need to do a little research to deduce which mode is better for you.

# Installing Cubase on Your Computer

The process of installing Cubase on your computer is virtually identical between the Mac and PC versions. However, there are a few differences I will reveal. Installation is very simple process, and the Cubase installer will prompt you through most steps. Therefore, I will not take you through the entire process, but rather some of the important steps that might require a bit more forethought.

To start the installation process, you'll need to insert your Cubase installation DVD into your optical drive. When you insert the disc, it will appear on your desktop (Mac) or on the Computer page (on Windows, click on the Start button, then click on Computer).

**BD-ROM Drive (G:) Cubase 6**
0 bytes free of 5.53 GB
UDF

Figure 1.3: The Cubase Install DVD icon

Double-click on that icon to launch the Start Center.

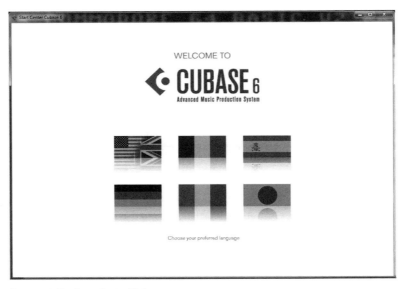

Figure 1.4: The Start Center Welcome screen

The Start Center Welcome screen will appear, prompting you to click on a flag to choose the preferred language. After clicking on a flag, the Installation screen will appear.

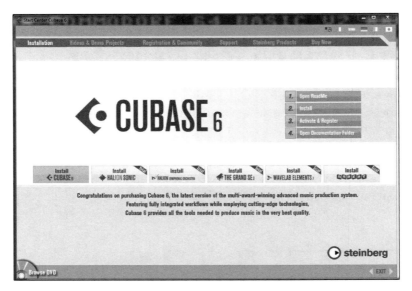

Figure 1.5: The Installation screen

At the upper left-hand side of the screen, you will find the Installation tab. Underneath and slightly below the center of the screen, you will find the installers. Make sure you currently have the Install Cubase 6 button selected. (The other installers offer trial versions of the full HALion Sonic, HALion Symphonic Orchestra, The Grand SE3, WaveLab Elements 7, and REBEAT. You may install these optional trial programs; however, none of them are required for using this book.)

Located in the upper right-hand corner of the Installation screen are the four "install steps" buttons. I would recommend clicking on the Open ReadMe button. (You will be prompted about installing Acrobat Reader if it is not currently on your computer.) Within the ReadMe file is very detailed information about the installation process. If you need further installation details, refer to this ReadMe file.

Click on the Install button. (Step button 2.)

This will launch the Cubase installer. From here, the installation process will prompt you through a very straightforward set of steps. But PC users will be presented with this window:

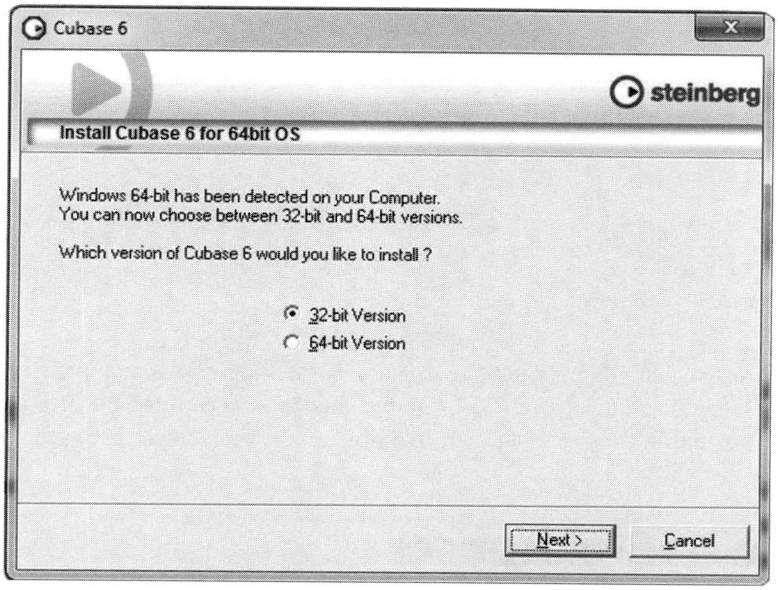

Figure 1.6: 32-bit or 64-bit-mode installer

This is the screen that allows 64-bit Microsoft Windows users to choose which mode(s) to install. (If your Windows version is 32-bit, you will not see this screen.) As I stated previously, I prefer to install both modes, which requires two separate installations procedures: one for the 32-bit mode version and another for the 64-bit version. (See "32-Bit or 64-Bit Mode for Windows PC Users" earlier in this chapter.)

Note: During the process, you may notice the installation of a program called the eLicenser Control Center. This is software that runs the USB-eLicenser (see "Using the USB-eLicenser" later in this chapter) and is required to run Cubase on your computer. Please allow the entire installation of that program.

After the installation process completes, there are still some tasks you must perform before you can start using Cubase. To that end, please continue with this chapter.

# Enabling 64-Bit Mode on a Mac

When you install Cubase, it is configured for 32-bit mode by default. So if you want to run Cubase in 64-bit mode, you must alter its configuration. It's a fairly simple thing to do. From the Finder, click on the Go menu and select Applications. A window will appear with a list of all the applications installed on the computer. Single-click on the Cubase icon, then click on the File menu and select Get Info.

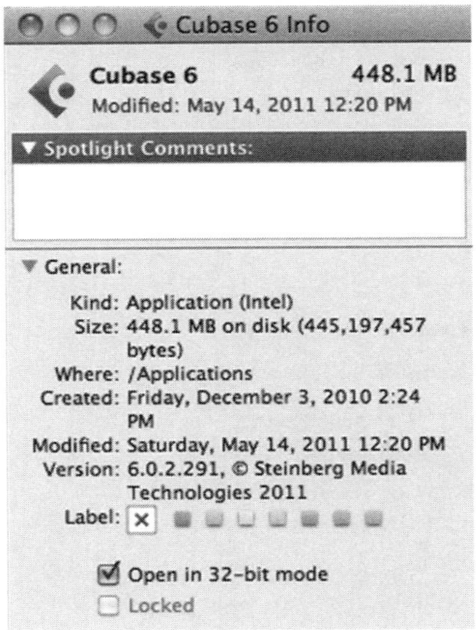

Figure 1.7: The Cubase 6 Info window

In the General area (which you may have to expand by clicking on the triangle next to "General"), you'll see that the Open in 32-bit mode checkbox is enabled by default. Uncheck that box to enable Cubase to launch in 64-bit mode, then close the window and launch Cubase normally.

# Using the USB-eLicenser

If you purchased Cubase for the first time, then the USB-eLicenser was in the box. If you've purchased an upgrade from a previous or lower version of Cubase, then you probably have a USB-eLicenser and know what it's all about. But for those who haven't worked with hardware copy protection before, let me help you understand what it is and how to use it.

Figure 1.8: The USB-eLicenser

Note: Cubase and Cubase Artist use the USB-eLicenser, while Cubase Elements uses a Soft-eLicenser that installs a software license upon your computer.

At first glance, the USB-eLicenser is easily mistaken for a USB flash drive or "thumb drive." Instead of containing computer documents such as photos and word-processor files, the USB-eLicenser contains the license for Cubase. That license must be downloaded and installed on the USB-eLicenser before you can start using Cubase. (See "Entering Your Activation Code" on the next page.)

The USB-eLicenser is also known as a "dongle." Dongles have been around since the early days of high-performance software. It is a copy-protection device. Without the USB-eLicenser connected to a USB port of your computer, Cubase will not run. Think of it as the keys to your car; if you don't have the key, you won't be able to start the car. Suffice it to say, the USB-eLicenser is a very important component in your Cubase-equipped studio.

Instead of having a protracted discussion of the pros and cons of software copy protection, let me say this: of all the copy-protection schemes (serial number, challenge/response, etc.), I like the USB-eLicenser the best. (Or perhaps I should say I dislike it the least?) It allows me to install Cubase on *all* of my computers. I regularly use Cubase on nine different Macs and PCs. All I have to do is plug the USB-eLicenser into the computer I'll be using, and away I go. Other schemes allow installation on only two computers. In my case, that's a difficult proposition. The biggest advantage to the USB-eLicenser is that it protects the future development of Cubase and the other Steinberg products I rely upon. Sure it's a drag, but so is learning a whole new program just because rampant piracy caused the demise of your trusted software. So not only does the USB-eLicenser protect Steinberg; it also protects your investment in the software and possibly your livelihood.

Every copy-protection scheme has idiosyncrasies, and the USB-eLicenser is no exception. With that in mind, let's talk about them so that you can avoid disaster. You must realize that it's a piece of hardware. Therefore, it can be forgotten, damaged, or lost. Any one of those possibilities will prevent you from launching Cubase and working on your music. That's why I strongly recommend registering your USB-eLicenser. Registration is the only way for Steinberg to verify that you are a registered user and therefore eligible for a replacement USB-eLicenser should yours become damaged or lost.

## Entering Your Activation Code

After you've installed Cubase or Cubase Artist, you'll need to download the license onto the USB-eLicenser. Or in the case of Cubase Elements, you'll need to download the Soft-eLicenser. Either way, you'll need to enter the activation code.

Note: Retail levels of Cubase and Cubase Artist ship with a USB-eLicenser with a twenty-five-day license. That allows you to start using Cubase right away and also gives you time to get to an Internet-connected computer. After the twenty-fifth day, you will need to download a license, as outlined in these instructions.

The activation code is a 32-digit string of alphanumeric characters that can be found on a single sheet of paper contained in the Cubase box, or was sent to you in an email if you're upgrading. Either way, it's the activation code that allows you to download your Cubase license.

First, you must make sure you have the USB-eLicenser connected to a USB port of your computer. Next, run the eLicenser Control Center software.

Note: The license download process requires an Internet connection. If the computer with which you'll be using Cubase is not connected to the Internet, you'll need to install the eLicenser Control Center software onto a computer that has an Internet connection. Then you can connect the USB-eLicenser to that computer and download the license to it.

Mac users: From the Finder, choose the Go menu and select Applications. On the window that appears, double-click eLicenser Control Center.

Windows users: Click the Start button in the lower left-hand corner of the Windows desktop, then click Programs (XP) or All Programs (Vista, Windows 7). Then click on the eLicenser folder and select eLicenser Control Center.

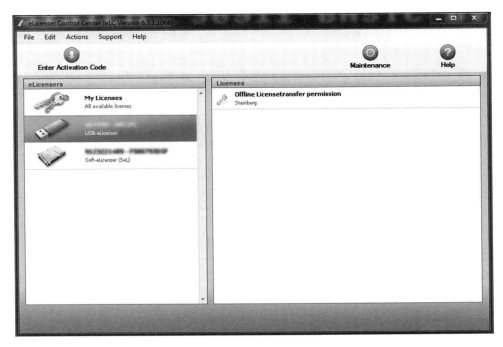

Figure 1.9: The eLicenser Control Center interface

Have your 32-digit code ready, and click on the Enter Activation Code button in the upper left-hand corner of the interface.

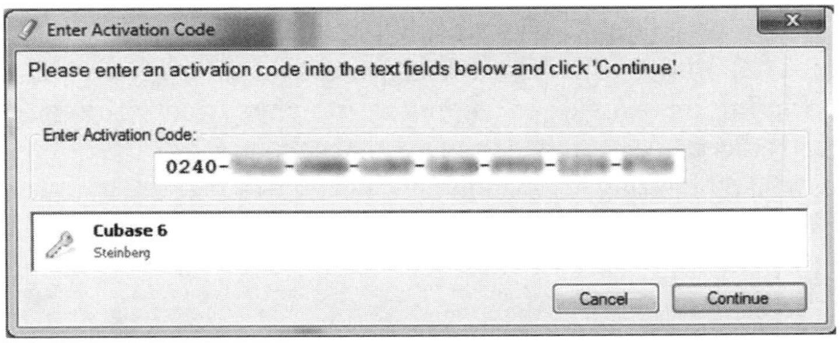

Figure 1.10: The Activation Code window

Enter the 32-digit code in the window. Every Steinberg code I've seen begins with "0240," but be very careful to enter the code precisely. Otherwise the license download will fail. When you enter the very last digit, the license type will appear in the bottom of the window. Click the Continue button to move on to the Select eLicenser window.

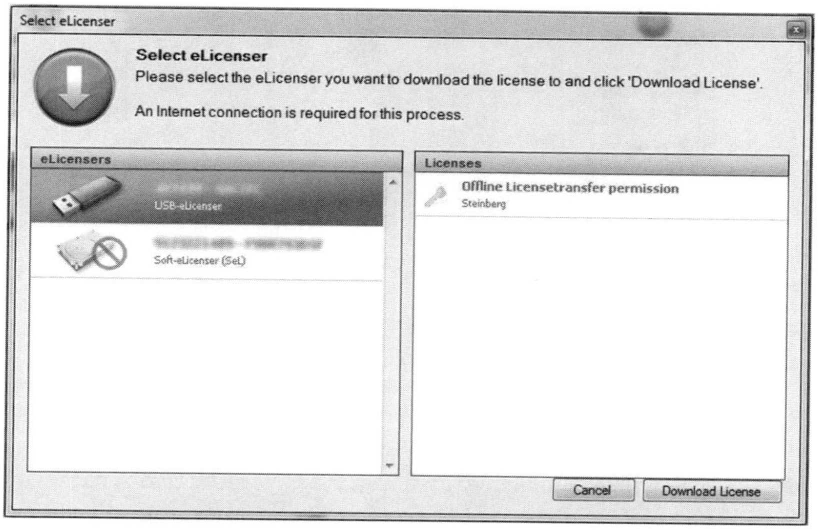

Figure 1.11: The Select eLicenser window

Most users will see both a USB-eLicenser and a Soft-eLicenser in this window. (If you don't see the former, make sure the USB-eLicenser is connected to the USB port of the computer and that the eLicenser Control Center software was installed properly. You may also need to remove and reattach the USB-eLicenser or reboot your computer.) Click on the USB-eLicenser on the left-hand side of the window, and then click on Download License. (If you have multiple USB-eLicensers, make sure to choose the one you wish the license to be downloaded to.) The License Download window will appear.

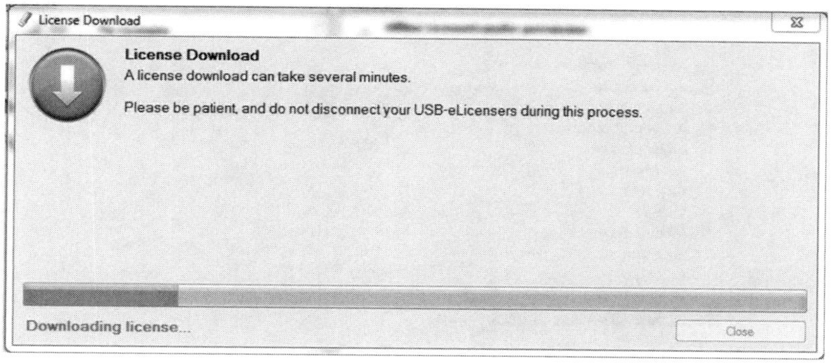

Figure 1.12: The License Download window

The directions say that the download can require several minutes. In my experience, it takes less than a minute. Nevertheless, follow the instructions on the window to be patient, and don't remove the USB-eLicenser.

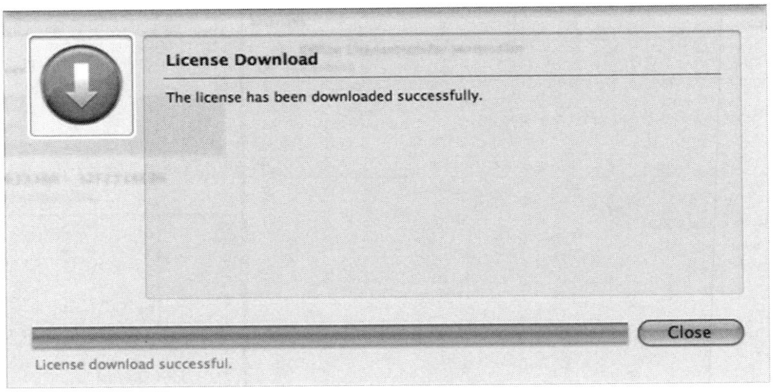

**License Download**

The license has been downloaded successfully.

Close

License download successful.

Figure 1.13: License Download Complete

After the license download is complete, you will receive a confirmation screen. You can now launch and start using Cubase. If you received an error message during the download, please try again, and make sure your computer is connected to the Internet.

# Adding Cubase to the "Dock" (Mac)

The "Dock" is located at the very bottom of your screen. It provides a very convenient way to launch Cubase quickly. However, you must add Cubase to the Dock manually.

From the Finder, click on the Go menu and select Applications. Locate the Cubase icon, click and drag the icon to your preferred position on the Dock, and then release the mouse button.

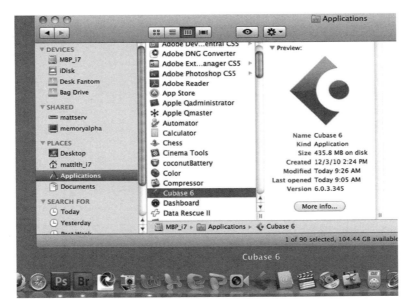

Figure 1.14: Adding Cubase to the Dock

Now you can launch Cubase by clicking on its icon in the Dock.

# "Pinning" Cubase to the Taskbar and Start Menu (Windows)

The Taskbar and Start menu are located in the lower left-hand corner of your screen. They provide a convenient way to launch Cubase quickly. However, you must add, or "pin," Cubase to the Dock manually. Plus, if you've installed both 32-bit and 64-bit versions of Cubase, you'll need to pin both versions.

From the Windows desktop, click on the Start button and then click on All Programs. Let's pin the 32-bit version of Cubase first by clicking on the Steinberg Cubase folder, and then right-click on the Cubase icon.

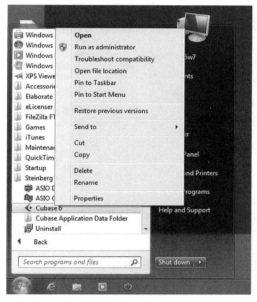

Figure 1.15: The Submenu with Pin Commands

Click on Pin to Taskbar, and then click on Pin to Start Menu. (The submenu should remain open during the operations.)

Now pin the 64-bit version by clicking on the Steinberg Cubase 64-bit folder, and then right-click on the Cubase icon. Click on the "Pin" commands described in the previous paragraph. When you're done, both 32-bit and 64-bit icons will be added to both the Taskbar and the Start menu.

If you installed both the 32-bit and 64-bit versions, I would recommend changing their names in the Start menu. Click on the Start button to reveal the Start menu. You'll notice that the 32-bit version is named "Cubase," while the 64-bit version is named "Cubase (2)." Right-click on either icon, and select Properties from the submenu. The Properties window will appear. Click on the General tab, wherein you'll see the Cubase shortcut icon. To the right of the icon is a field into which you can enter the desired name. I would recommend something like "Cubase 32-bit" and "Cubase 64-bit," respectively. That way, you'll know which version of Cubase you'll be launching when you click on either icon.

Figure 1.16: The Taskbar and Start Menu with Cubase pinned within

The icons in the Taskbar do not have names, and they look identical. For this reason, you'll have to remember which version is on the left and which version is on the right.

# Creating a MySteinberg Account

As I mentioned previously in this chapter, creating a MySteinberg account and registering your software is very important. Steinberg has made this process fairly simple. First, the computer from which you're registering must be connected to the Internet. Next, from the Installation tab of the Start Center, select Step 3: Activate and Register. (See Figure 1.5.) Or if you've already put away your installation DVD, you can also launch Cubase, and then close the Project Assistant window when it appears. The Registration Reminder window will appear.

Figure 1.17: The Registration Reminder window

On the window, you can choose from Register Now, Already Registered, and Remind me later! (Notice also that you can get back to the Registration Reminder screen at any time by clicking on the Help menu and selecting Registration.)

Due to the importance of registering, I would recommend you take a few minutes and do so now. Using either the Start Center or Registration Reminder window will take you to the MySteinberg page at www.steinberg.net. There you will find more information about downloading a license and the registration process.

## Entering Your eLicenser Serial Number

During the registration process, you'll be asked to enter the serial number of either your USB-eLicenser or, in the case of Cubase Elements, your Soft-eLicenser. There are a couple of little tricks I've learned that can help you streamline this process.

First, you need to know that the twelve- or thirteen-digit USB-eLicenser serial numbers are case sensitive. Make sure you always use capital letters when entering the serial number.

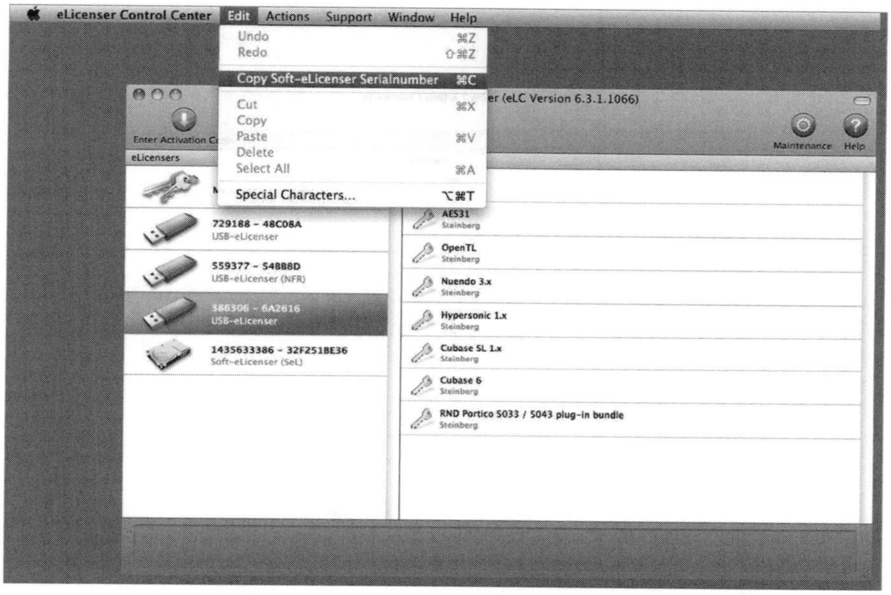

Figure 1.18: The Copy Soft-eLicenser Serialnumber command

Second, Soft-eLicenser serial numbers are up to twenty digits long. To aid in accurate entry of the digits, you can launch the eLicenser Control Center program, click on the Edit menu, and then select Copy Soft-eLicenser Serialnumber.

Then return to the registration page and use a paste command to paste the digits into the serial number field.

# Upgrading from Cubase Artist to Cubase

One of the greatest things Steinberg has added to Cubase 6 is the speed with which you can upgrade from Cubase 6 Artist to Cubase 6. During the Cubase Artist installation process, all of the software necessary to run full Cubase was already installed. Therefore, all you need to do is purchase an upgrade code at the shop on www. steinberg.net. Using that code will allow you to download the Cubase 6 upgrade via the eLicenser Control Center. That means you don't have to wait for the upgrade while it's being shipped to you. Plus if you find a feature of Cubase that would be beneficial for your music production, you can upgrade from Cubase Artist at any time, day or night.

# Almost Ready to Launch

Since you've completed the installation, activation, and registration processes, I'm sure you're excited to launch Cubase and start your music production. You could certainly do so at this time. However, in the next chapter, I'll be offering some really important information about other hardware, such as audio interfaces, microphones, and MIDI devices. Plus there will be really important information about how to use this book to its full potential and how to set up your studio for proper monitoring. Reading the next chapter will help you get started with Cubase the right way—the first time.

# Chapter 2
# HARDWARE AND STUDIO CONFIGURATION

A modern recording studio can be defined as a physical structure full of recording equipment. It can also be defined as a city bus while you have your laptop open and are mixing music on your way home from work. But regardless of whether your studio is brick and mortar or simply a laptop running Cubase, the process of recording still relies heavily on hardware. In the last chapter, we talked about a very important piece of hardware: the computer upon which you will run Cubase. But it doesn't end there. There are a myriad of hardware devices that are required for the recording process. You will be using some combination of microphones, keyboards, turntables, cables, and monitor speakers—most likely, all of the above. So this chapter is dedicated to choosing the right hardware for your purposes and configuring it to work with Cubase. In this chapter, you will learn about:

- Choosing an audio interface.
- Choosing microphones.
- Adding a MIDI controller or keyboard.
- Adding the right hardware for your music production needs.
- PC versus Mac modifier keys.
- Configuring your studio space.
- Proper monitoring of audio recordings.

## Choosing an Audio Interface

One of the most critical components in a DAW-based recording studio is the audio interface. It is the audio device through which you capture and monitor the recordings you're making. Most new DAW users make the easy mistake of trying to use their computers' built-in audio interfaces. Without going into a protracted discussion of why, the bottom line is that they're woefully inadequate for music production. Not only is the audio quality dubious, but also I've never seen a computer with high-quality XLR microphone preamps and phantom power. Suffice it to say, trying to use your computer's built-in audio interface will present you with challenges that are easily and inexpensively overcome by getting a high-quality audio interface.

There are a wide variety of different audio interfaces that you can use with Cubase. In fact, Steinberg is greatly responsible for the proliferation of high-performance audio interfaces. Steinberg created a technology called ASIO, which is an acronym for Audio Streaming Input/Output. It is a driver model that most audio-interface manufacturers adopted, due to its robust design and the fact that Steinberg made the ASIO technology license free. Therefore, all audio-interface manufacturers could create ASIO-compatible hardware without having to pay Steinberg for the technology. The outcome has been a veritable cornucopia of high-quality, highly specialized audio interfaces from which to choose.

With that variety comes the challenge of choosing the right one. But I can help you decide by introducing you to my method of choosing an interface. I recommend that you use my S.F.P. criteria, for it can quickly narrow the selection and help you choose the best audio interface for your purposes.

## The S.F.P. Criteria

S.F.P. is an acronym for Sound, Features, and Price and should be used in that order (sound being the most important point and price being the least). The criteria are very useful no matter what audio commodity you're buying. I've used it to purchase everything from cables to audio interfaces, even for instruments. Once you've used it, you'll see how it can help you choose the right device. But in this case, let's use it to choose the right audio interface for you.

### Sound

Finding the audio interface with the right sound is usually the most challenging of the criteria to determine. How an interface sounds could be defined either by sound quality or sound character. I feel it should define both. The quality and variety of mic preamps (microphone preamplifiers) and AD/DA (analog-to-digital/digital-to-analog) convertors has never been higher. Put simply, it's difficult to find a bad-sounding third-party audio interface these days. Therefore, it's better to base your sound criteria on character rather than quality.

The most popular audio interfaces on the market today have their own mic preamps. Having the preamps onboard allows you to plug microphones directly into the audio interface without the need for additional hardware such as a mixer or separate mic preamp. Therefore, having built-in mic preamps not only saves you money but also makes recording more convenient and less noisy.

Since audio interfaces are digital, you will have to make sure that the one you choose has appropriately high-performance digital specifications. Look for an interface that is at least 24-bit and has a sample frequency of at least 44.1 kHz. The amplitude of sound is measured in digital bits, while the frequencies of sound are measured by the sample frequency. In either case, the higher the numbers, the better chance you have of capturing the essence of the sound you're recording.

Some of you might be hoping for me to reveal the best-sounding audio interface with the best-sounding mic preamps. However, the subjective nature of how each of us perceives sound makes that determination impossible. In other words, I could no more accurately determine which mic preamp sounds best than I could which bass guitar sounds best, which country album sounds best, and which seventeenth-century composer wrote the best sounding baroque music. I could certainly answer those questions (Status; Johnny Cash: *At Folsom Prison*; J. S. Bach), but I'm making those judgments based only on what *I* hear with *my* ears. Since I don't have your ears, I cannot predict what you would define as the best-sounding anything, let alone an audio interface.

The easy answer to this question is the same as the answer to most recording questions: use your ears. Sit down with an audio interface, and really listen to the recording and the playback of your music. Use microphones you're familiar with, and listen in your studio through your speakers. Then, and only then, can you truly determine the audio interface with best sound character and sound quality. For example, I went to my local music store, and they let me borrow five popular audio interfaces. (Yes, a significant yet refundable down payment was required.) I spent the evening recording and the morning listening to each one. Which interface did I feel sounded the best?

Figure 2.1: The Steinberg MR816CSX audio interface

I found the Steinberg MR816CSX to be the best-sounding audio interface of the bunch. It has very unique-sounding D-Pre (Darlington) mic preamps. They're not the flattest-sounding preamps you'll ever hear (flat rarely sounds good), but they have an extraordinary sonic character. That being said, recording and listening to a variety of audio interfaces will help you determine which one sounds best to you.

## Features

After you've found a great-sounding audio interface, you'll need to determine if it has the features you'll need. The list of features on a modern audio interface varies widely. However, I'll tell you about the three most critical features to consider.

The first is number of discrete input channels. The number of input channels will determine how many discrete tracks you can record simultaneously. For example, a Steinberg CI2 interface has two inputs.

Figure 2.2: The Steinberg CI2+ audio interface

That will allow you to record one stereo track (such as the output of a synthesizer) or up to two mono inputs (such as a mic and guitar) simultaneously. When I'm working on my solo projects, I rarely need to record with more than one or two inputs.

But there are situations that require more than two inputs to be recorded simultaneously. For example, a drum set would normally require at least three inputs (kick drum, left overhead, and right overhead) and usually much more to capture each drum instrument on its own discrete track. A five-piece drum set normally requires kick, snare, hi-hat, tom 1, tom 2, floor tom, overhead left, and overhead right. That's a total of eight inputs all recorded simultaneously. If that's the case, you'll need to find an interface that features eight discrete inputs. The Steinberg MR816CSX is such an interface.

The next feature is compatibility. If you find a great-sounding interface such as the Apogee Duet *and* you use a Windows PC, you should be aware that the Duet (like most Apogee interfaces) are Mac only.

Figure 2.3: The Apogee Duet audio interface

Make sure the audio interface you're considering is compatible with your computer platform.

The last feature to consider is connectivity. In other words, how will the interface connect to your computer, and how will the devices you wish to record connect to the interface? Let's talk about the first part of that equation. Audio interfaces connect to a computer by one of three methods: USB, FireWire, or PCI. The former two allow you to easily move the device from one computer to another and are by far the most popular types of computer connectivity. The latter uses a card slot inside of the computer, which can be higher performance at the cost of portability. Just make sure that the interface that you're considering can connect to your computer.

Now let's consider audio connectivity. That is being able to connect all of the devices you plan to record.

Figure 2.4: S/PDIF and ADAT Ports on the Steinberg MR816CSX

For example, if you're capturing digital data from a DAT (Digital Audio Tape) recorder, you'll need an interface with S/PDIF (Sony/Philips Digital Interface Format) or AES/EBU (Audio Engineering Society/European Broadcasting Union) input ports. Or if you're using a mic preamp (such as the Presonus DigiMax D8) with an ADAT optical interface (a.k.a. lightpipe) connection, make sure the interface you're considering also has an ADAT optical interface.

### Price

Price is the easiest of the criteria with which to choose an audio interface: if you can't afford it, it won't help you make any music. That might sound harsh, but it's the truth. Fortunately we live in an age where quality and functionality goes up, while at the same time, cost comes down. Today's modern audio interfaces can cost one hundred dollars or less. Of course, some of the more potent interfaces can run several hundred dollars. But by using the S.F.P. criteria, you will be able to find a great-sounding interface that serves you well at a price you can afford.

# Additional Hardware Requirements

An audio interface is just one piece of hardware you'll need. There are others, so I'd like to go over a few. Bear in mind that you may not need all of the following items. For example, if you're not recording "real" instruments (such as acoustic guitars, vocals, or trumpets), then you won't need microphones. However, there are some items that are absolutely necessary for music production.

## Microphones

If you plan to capture sound from acoustic devices such as vocals and guitars, then you will certainly need a number of microphones. The importance of high-quality microphones cannot be overstated. Microphones are the "ears" of your recordings. In fact, many of the "British invasion" records (such as those by the Beatles and the Who) still hold up to today's audio standards simply because the microphones used during the recording process were exceptionally good. A great microphone recorded on average equipment will always sound better than an average microphone recorded on great equipment. The rule is: unless your budget is extremely limited, never, ever, *ever* skimp on microphones.

It's also important to consider the instrument you're recording before choosing which microphone to record it with. For example, I'm a big fan of the Audio Technica AT4033/CL side address microphone. In fact, I own four of them. It's a very affordable, wonderful-sounding general-purpose microphone when recording vocals, acoustic guitars, brass, strings, woodwinds, and more. However, I wouldn't recommend it on snare drum, bass drum, or guitar amp, nor would I use it for live-performance vocal recording. For those applications, you'd be better served by choosing a microphone specially designed for those purposes.

Another important recommendation is this: unless you simply can't afford a recording microphone, don't try to record vocals with a live-performance microphone such as a Shure SM58 or other handheld model. While they sound good on the stage and are of rugged design, they are ill suited for vocal capture in a recording studio.

Getting a good pop filter will also help you keep the unavoidable "plosives" in consonants such as "power" and "popular" from overloading the microphone. Steadman makes some truly innovative metal designs that tame the plosives without coloring the sound.

I would recommend reading *Hal Leonard Recording Method—Book One: Microphones and Mixers* for a thoughtful tutorial on choosing recording microphones.

## Studio Monitors

Studio monitor speakers are another critical component to your modern recording studio. Unlike consumer-grade speakers, studio monitors are designed to accurately reproduce an average or "flat" sounding recording. The idea is that if you can make a good-sounding mix on average speakers, the mix will sound even better when played on consumer speakers.

Many new DAW users will be tempted to mix with headphones or consumer speakers they already own. Doing so is an understandable yet profound mistake! Many unwitting users will waste hours mixing and remixing their music, because while it sounds great on their consumer speakers, it sounds terrible on their car stereo or MP3 player. To spare you from this fate, spend some time at your local music store listening to different studio monitors. Take a combination of your own music along with some of your favorite CDs. That way, you'll be able to judge the studio monitors by listening to music you're familiar with. Try and do it during the day and not on a weekend; otherwise the salespeople will be busy and your ears will be competing with some guy playing the opening riff to "Crazy Train," over and over and over …

## Headphones

While you cannot accurately mix on them, headphones are critical when recording acoustic instruments or vocals. The rule is that musicians must be able to hear a mix of their performances and previously recorded tracks. However, if the mix is being played back through speakers, the microphones will record that sound along with the desired sound. This phenomenon is known as a "feedback loop." Not only will it negatively impact the recording, but it will also result in obnoxious squealing and howling if the volume becomes too loud. Either way, your tracks will be ruined.

Instead, the musicians must wear headphones. They'll be able to hear the mix and their instruments without the sound being looped back into the microphone. I would recommend getting a pair of closed-back headphones. Open-back designs might leak sound back into the microphone and could also be prone to high-pitched squealing feedback. Try and get headphones with large diaphragms. They produce richer bass and are easier for a musician to use in a "one-off" configuration (one cuff on the ear, the other cuff off).

Another consideration during the mixing process is determining how the mix will sound on consumer headphones. It's a good idea to take those earbuds that came with your iPod (or other "i" device) and listen to your mix through those. They are certainly not the pinnacles of headphone fidelity, but they will allow you to hear your music as it will be heard by the public who use those ubiquitous small, white earbuds.

## MIDI Controller and/or MIDI Interface

If you're planning to use MIDI or VST (virtual) Instrument tracks, you'll need a MIDI controller with which to enter the data. If you have a keyboard-equipped synthesizer, you're all set. Such a synthesizer would have either MIDI ports or a built-in USB MIDI interface. But if cost and/or portability are important, you may want to consider a dedicated controller design with an onboard USB port. Dedicated controllers have no sound of their own, relying instead on the sounds generated by Cubase or instrument plug-ins. They plug directly into your computer's USB port, so no dedicated MIDI interface will be required. Since they lack their own internal sound-generation hardware, controllers are more affordable, and they come in a wide variety of keyboard and pad-style designs. I carry a small twenty-five-note controller in my "go" bag so that I can record MIDI tracks when I'm on the road. A visit to your local music store will reveal numerous MIDI controllers in every configuration and price range. Checking out the offerings from Alesis, Akai, and Arturia would be a good place to start.

However, if your keyboard or controller does not have its own USB port, you might need to invest in a dedicated MIDI interface. Before you do, determine if your audio interface has MIDI ports (in, out). If it does, you can use those to establish MIDI communication between Cubase and your external MIDI controller. Otherwise, you'll need a USB-to-MIDI interface: basically, a converter with a USB port on one end and MIDI ports on the other. If you have multiple MIDI devices without their own USB ports, the MIDI interface you choose should be of a multiport design. Such interfaces would have only one USB port but have two, four, six, or more MIDI ports and spare you from purchasing a separate interface for every MIDI device.

# Keeping Up to Date

The speed at which music technology evolves is staggering. Add to that the rapid pace of operating-system and hardware development, and you have a recipe for crashes and operational weirdness. To minimize the chances of getting detoured by such an event, I strongly recommend that you keep all of your software and hardware up to date. If your computer is connected to the Internet, both Macs and Windows PCs will update themselves with your approval. However, programs such as Cubase and eLicenser Control Center will require a manual update process. Visit both www.steinberg.net and www.elicenser.net for the most up-to-date program versions.

Your other computer hardware (including but not limited to audio and MIDI interfaces) comes with driver software that connects the devices to the operating system and Cubase. Those drivers are usually found on an installer disc that came in the box. However, I strongly recommend that you not install those drivers without checking the manufacturer's website for the most current drivers. You see, the disc in the box got shipped, stored, stocked, and possibly even reshipped before you received it. Therefore, it will probably contain obsolete drivers. Out-of-date drivers are notorious for causing a myriad of computer problems. For that reason, visit the website of your audio and MIDI interfaces regularly, and make sure you download and install the most current drivers. (This practice is prudent for all computer hardware, including printers, scanners, cameras, mice, smart phones, etc.)

# Windows, Macs, Mice, and Modifiers

Cubase is cross-platform, meaning that it runs on both Windows and Mac operating systems. That's great for you, but it makes it more challenging when writing or reading this book because of the differences between mice and keyboards. I've come up with a simple way to streamline the deceptions of operations that are mouse- or keyboard-centric.

## Using and Enabling Right-Click on a Mac

There are a lot of functions in Cubase that are accessed by right-clicking your mouse. That's an easy proposition for Windows users, because their mice have two buttons: one for left and one for right. However, Apple hardware only has one mouse button, which makes right-clicking a little harder. By default, Mac users will need to hold the Ctrl key on their keyboards and then click on something to reveal the right-click submenu. However, you can enable your Apple-branded mouse or (MacBook, MacBook Pro, MacBook Air) trackpad to use right-click. Those settings are located in the System Preferences under the Apple logo menu in the upper left-hand corner of your screen.

Click on Mouse and/or Trackpad in the Hardware row, and enable the secondary click options for right-click. That way, when you read "right-click" in this book, you'll be able to access the right-click submenus with your mouse instead of having to Ctrl-click.

Over the past few years, Apple has been including little videos in the Mouse and Trackpad control panels that show you the "gestures." While you're configuring your secondary click options, have a peak at the videos, for they will help instruct you on how to use gestures. (You may need to consult the manual that came with your Mac for further details.)

## Key Commands and Modifier Keys

Key commands (a.k.a. keyboard shortcuts) can make short work of commonly used software operations. Instead of relying on using your mouse to select a menu, drag down the list, select an operation, and finally click on OK, a key command allows you to execute the operation simply by typing a key (or series of keys) on your computer keyboard. I'm a firm believer in key commands, and this book will show you how to use them.

However, a standard computer keyboard wouldn't offer many key commands without the invention of modifier keys. Those are the keys that work in combination with the standard keys to expand the number of key combinations.

A Windows PC has the following modifier keys:

- Shift
- Control (Ctrl)
- Alternate (Alt)

An Apple Macintosh has the following modifier keys:

- Shift
- Control (Ctrl)
- Option
- Command (⌘)

You can see that both platforms share the Shift key, so that modifier is interchangeable. The Ctrl (Control) key is also found on both platforms; however, it is *not* interchangeable. Most cross-platform applications (such as Cubase) interchange the Windows Ctrl key with the Mac Command key. I know that can be confusing. To that end, let me show you how I'll be indicating the modifier keys.

The Copy operation on a Windows PC is: Ctrl + C. That is to say, to execute a copy, press and hold the Ctrl key and then type the "C" key on your computer keyboard. (Note: the "+" in the key command indicates a combination of modifier and key, not actually typing the "+" key.)

The Copy operation on an Apple Macintosh is: Command + C. That is to say, to execute a copy, press and hold the Command key and then type the "C" key on your computer keyboard. (See the note about the "+" indicator in the previous paragraph.)

Now let me show you how the Copy operation will be indicated in this book:

- Ctrl/Command + C

Notice that the Windows modifier (Ctrl) comes first, while the Mac modifier comes second (Command) separated by a "/." That is the way it shall be throughout this book. However, in the case where unique modifiers are used with the interchangeable Shift key, the key command will appear as:

- Shift + Ctrl/Command + L

That is to say, pressing and holding both the Shift and the related PC/Mac modifier key, then typing the "L" key, will execute the operation. In this case, it's the Lock operation.

## "F" or Function Keys

Some of the most commonly used Cubase key commands are located on the function keys of your computer keyboard. The function keys appear above the number keys of your QWERTY keyboard. They're usually labeled—F1 through F12, or in some cases there will be up to F19 or more. If you're using Windows, it's most likely that you can just type the key to access the key command. For example, typing F3 will make the Cubase mixer visible, F4 will display VST Connections, and F11 will display the VST Instruments rack. Easy, right?

### Function Keys on a Mac

Well it's not quite as easy on a Mac, at least not yet. You see, the Mac OS reserves the function buttons for everyday Mac operations. For example, typing F3, F4, and F11 (depending on the vintage of your Mac keyboard) will activate Exposé, Dashboard, and volume Mute respectively. Therefore you'll need to know how to access the function keys when you see them throughout this book.

Figure 2.5: The "fn" key on a Mac keyboard

There are two ways make the Mac function keys into the actual function keys. One method is to locate the "fn" button on your Mac keyboard. Holding the fn key and then typing a function key will allow you to access the prescribed Cubase key commands.

This method might work best for you if you're a casual Cubase user or rely on the Mac commands during your daily computer use. However, if you are using Cubase a lot (and I sincerely hope you are), I would recommend changing the function key behavior from within the Mac OS. Click on the Apple menu, and select System Preferences. Then locate the hardware row, and click on Keyboard.

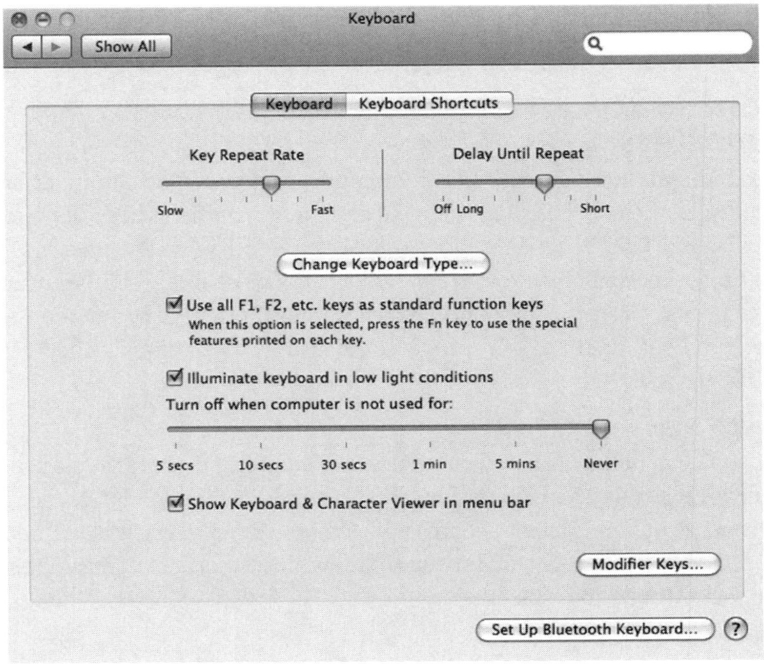

Figure 2.6: The Keyboard Preferences window

Make sure the Keyboard tab is selected at the top of the window. When you enable the "Use all F1, F2, etc. keys as standard function keys" option, then most of the function keys will operate as function keys rather than Mac functions. That way you won't have to hold the fn key to access the Cubase key commands assigned to the function keys. However, there is one other setting you should disable. Click on the Keyboard Shortcuts tab at the top of the window.

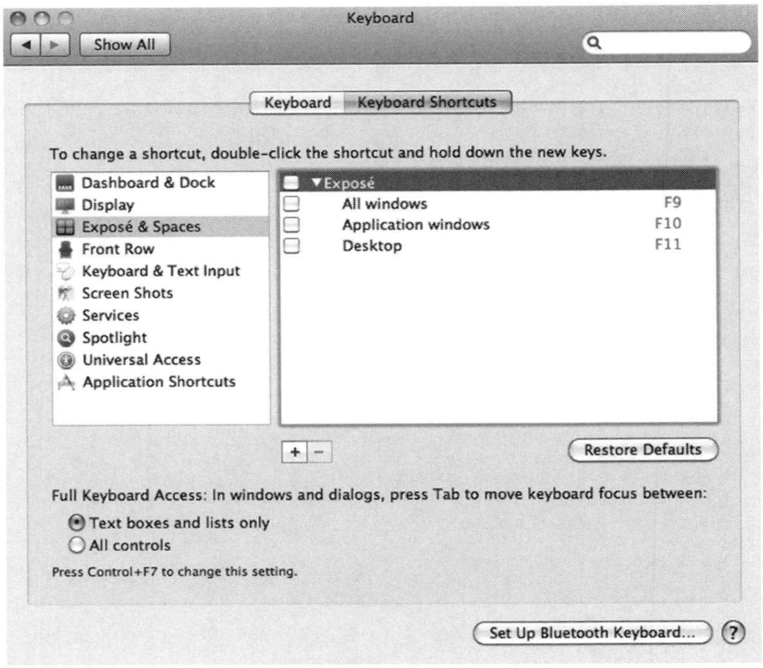

Figure 2.7: The Keyboard Shortcuts Preferences window

On the left side of the window, click on Exposé and Spaces, then disable Exposé on the right-hand side. The three additional Exposé keys (All windows, Application windows, and Desktop) will be disabled when you disable Exposé. Close the window when finished.

# Your Studio Setup

The setup of your studio equipment is paramount to your work flow. Not only can it speed up your rate of production, but it can also critically affect what you're hearing. And since music is about being able to communicate with sound, you'll really need to hear what's going on in your mix. To that end, let me offer some advice on how to arrange your equipment and why.

## Arranging Your Studio Monitors

There is a very simple and effective method for arranging your stereo studio monitor. (Note: This method is for stereo monitors. Surround-sound configurations are much different.) By using the "triangle" method I'm about to show you, you'll be able to get the most accurate representation of your mix. Failure to use this method will make it more difficult or even impossible to really hear what's going on.

Imagine an equilateral triangle with one point at the center of your head and the other two points touching the center of each studio monitor. Believe it or not, this represents 98 percent of the calculations you'll have to make for proper studio-monitor setup.

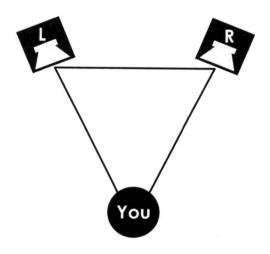

Figure 2.8: Overhead view of the "triangle" method

The diagram above (that admittedly resembles a grade school geometry lesson) depicts an overhead view of the equilateral triangle. You can see the left speaker and right speaker and your head. Basically, the distance between the speakers should be the same as the distance between the left speaker and your left ear, and the right speaker and your right ear. You should also consider angling the speaker toward your head a few degrees. That degree is exaggerated in Figure 2.8, but avoid pointing the studio monitors flush toward the back of the room.

The height of the speakers should ideally be equal to the height of your ears when sitting (I'm assuming you're not one of those "stand while mixing" types) in front of the speakers. However, I've found that situation more difficult to achieve. Every studio I've ever been in has, due to practicality, put their studio monitors higher than ear height. Then, tilting the monitors towards the engineer's head completes the optimal speaker configuration. This is a perfectly acceptable way to arrange your studio monitors. If you have a desk that raises the height of your monitors above your ears, consider getting some Auralex MoPADs (www.auralex.com). They not only allow you to tilt the speakers toward your head but also help isolate the speakers from the desk.

## Woe to the Ears of a Musician

In an episode of *Star Trek: The Next Generation*, Counselor Troi was driven mad by a song placed in her subconscious. She could hear it, but others could not. This situation is identical to a condition known as tinnitus. We've all experienced tinnitus at one time or another, usually after attending a loud concert or other event involving higher-than-average sound-pressure levels. The ears ring for a period of time, after which it disappears.

But imagine if that ringing in your ears were permanent. You'd hear it from the time you woke up to the time you tried to go to sleep. It would drive you mad too. Well, if you damage your hearing due to excessive exposure to loud music, you won't just have a diminished frequency response; you'll also have tinnitus. You won't be able to stop it; earplugs and hearing aids won't help; there is no therapy, no magic pill, and no cure. Once you have it, it's a life sentence.

The only way to keep from suffering the tortures of tinnitus is to reduce the volume and limit your exposure to loud music. I know we're all guilty of wanting to "crank it up" when we feel the need. But if you exercise some caution, you'll be able to not only enjoy music throughout your life but also cherish the sound of raindrops, a good night's sleep, and the gentle stirrings of your grandchildren.

To that end, be aware that the optimal average volume level when mixing music should not exceed 85 dB (decibels). I strongly recommend obtaining an SPL (Sound Pressure Level) meter with a slow or RMS (Root Mean Squared) response setting. If you have an iPhone, iPad, or iPod Touch, you can also download the Decibel Meter Pro 2 for $0.99 from the App Store. It may not be as accurate as a dedicated SPL meter. But I've tried the two side by side, and the Decibel Meter Pro 2 is extremely similar in response to my rather expensive SPL meter. More information can be found at www.performanceaudio.com.

## Keeping Your Equipment Handy and Close

Every so often, I visit clients' studios and am amazed by how far apart they have their components arranged. For example, the computer running Cubase is at one end of the room, while the MIDI controller is on the opposite side. From an aesthetic standpoint, it might look great. However, if the person doing the recording were also the keyboardist, he or she would have to run back and forth across the room several times (or in my keyboard skill–deficient case, several hundred times) during the recording process. That situation would be frustrating and distracting for the user and uncomplementary for the production workflow.

Instead, I would recommend you keep your instruments and other equipment as close together as possible. I like to keep my gear at arm's length. That way, I can have everything at my fingertips, and I'm not needlessly running around the room while I'm working. I also prefer to not lose a magical musical moment because I'm wrangling gear from all corners of the room.

## Moving Out of the Basement

Speaking of the corners of a room, we've laid the foundation of our new relationship with Cubase. Now it's time to move out of the basement and start adding the framework by launching Cubase for the first time.

# Chapter 3
# Launching Cubase for the First Time

Launching a deep program like Cubase can be both exciting and a little scary. Hopefully you've read the previous chapters, for if you have, excitement will more quickly allay any fears. Also, if you read the introduction to this book, you'll start seeing some of the numbered "Cubasics" I mentioned. Cubasics are significant operations, settings, and procedures that must become part of your operational relationship with Cubase. The sooner you memorize and implement the Cubasics, the faster you will become proficient with the program.

Before proceeding, you will need to make sure that you've installed Cubase and the eLicenser Control Center software, installed the drivers for your audio interface and MIDI interface (if necessary), connected your audio and MIDI interfaces to your computer, and connected the USB-eLicenser to a USB port of your computer. Then you can continue on to this chapter, in which you will learn about:

- Configuring your audio and MIDI interfaces.
- The WiFi and network activity factor.
- Eliminating a common source of hum and buzz.
- The Project Assistant window.
- Using proper media management.
- Setting up Auto Save.

## Go for Launch

In chapter 1, you learned how to add the Cubase program to your Start Menu or Taskbar (Windows PC) or to your Dock (Mac). Go ahead and launch Cubase by clicking on one of those icons. The first thing you'll see is the Cubase splash screen.

Figure 3.1: The Cubase splash screen

There are two items to pay attention to on the splash screen. The first is the version number of Cubase you currently have installed, along with the current memory address mode (See "Deciding to Run Cubase in 32-Bit or 64-Bit Mode," chapter 1). While you needn't do it every time, do periodically compare the version number to that of the most current version on the Steinberg website. (See "Keeping Up to Date, chapter 2.)

The second is the progress display. As Cubase initializes its core program components, hardware devices, and plug-ins (including third-party plug-ins, if you have any) they will appear in the progress display. It also tests the plug-ins to make sure they're Cubase-compatible.

When the initialization process is complete, the splash screen will disappear, and you'll see the Project Assistant window. However, we won't be going over the Project Assistant yet. Before we can proceed, we'll need to configure our MIDI and audio interfaces. So at this time, click the Cancel button on the Project Assistant window. If you see the registration reminders, take a moment to register. (See "Creating a MySteinberg Account," chapter 1.) Now locate the Devices menu.

# Configuring Your MIDI Interface

Click on the Devices menu and select Device Setup at the bottom. You will then see the Device Setup window. If this is the first time you've opened the Device Setup window, then the first selection in the Devices column will be MIDI Port Setup. If it is not, click on it to select it. There are slight differences between the MIDI Port Setup on Windows and the Mac, so I will show both.

| I/O | Port System Name | Show As | Visible | State | In 'All MIDI |
|---|---|---|---|---|---|
| In | Keystation Port 1 | Keystation Port 1 | ✕ | Active | ✕ |
| In | Network Session 1 | Network Session 1 | ✕ | Active | ✕ |
| In | Steinberg CI2 Port1 | Steinberg CI2 Port1 | ✕ | Active | ✕ |
| In | Taurus-3 Bass Pedal | Taurus-3 Bass Pedal | ✕ | Active | ✕ |
| Out | Keystation Port 1 | Keystation Port 1 | ✕ | Inactive | |
| Out | Network Session 1 | Network Session 1 | ✕ | Active | |
| Out | Steinberg CI2 Port1 | Steinberg CI2 Port1 | ✕ | Active | |
| Out | Taurus-3 Bass Pedal | Taurus-3 Bass Pedal | ✕ | Inactive | |

Devices:
- MIDI
  - MIDI Port Setup
- Remote Devices
  - Mackie Control
  - Quick Controls
  - Steinberg CI2
- Transport
  - Record Time Max
  - Time Display
- Video
  - Video Player
- VST Audio System
  - Steinberg CI2
- VST System Link

Figure 3.2: The Device Setup/MIDI Port Setup window (Mac)

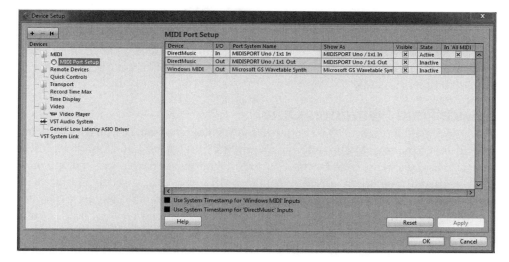

Figure 3.3: The Device Setup/MIDI Port Setup window (Windows)

The Device Setup window is divided into a left column labeled Devices and a right column that will display the settings for the selected device. In this case, the right column displays the settings for any and all MIDI interfaces you currently have connected to the computer. (Note: If the hardware is not currently connected, it will be absent from the right column. For the device to appear in the MIDI Port Setup window, you must quit Cubase, connect the hardware, and then restart Cubase.)

## The MIDI Port Setup Settings

The Devices column will display the settings for each connected interface. Figure 3.2 shows the settings of the four MIDI interfaces I have connected to my Mac: four In ports and four Out ports. The In port settings have a yellow background, while the Out port settings are blue. Figure 3.3 shows only one connected interface along with the default Windows MIDI Out port for the Microsoft GS Wavetable Synth. The background colorations are identical: yellow for In ports and blue for Out ports.

There won't be a need to learn about all of the MIDI Port Setup settings, but you should make sure that all of your interfaces appear in this window and that they all have their visible checkboxes enabled.

## Renaming the MIDI Ports

The Port System Name and Show As fields contain the same name. However, if you'd like to rename the ports, you can double-click in the Show As field and type in a new name. This is useful for truncating a verbose name or for identifying an external MIDI device connected to a port or interface. For example, in Figure 3.3, the name of the USB MIDI interface In port is "MIDISPORT UNO 1x1 In." I would be tempted to rename it "UNO IN."

Another suggestion would be to identify the port by the device to which it is connected rather than by the name of the interface. For example, if the UNO interface was connected to a Yamaha Motif synthesizer, I would probably change the Show As port names to "Motif IN" and "Motif OUT."

## The In "All MIDI Inputs" Checkbox

This in an important setting and is located at the far right of the Settings column. However, it may be difficult to find, because the default column width only allows for

In "All MIDI" to be displayed. Regardless of that idiosyncrasy, the setting is enabled on every In port by default. That allows you to record on a MIDI or Instrument track from any In port so that you don't necessarily have to change the Input setting of each track. We'll learn more about this later, but just make sure all of your In ports have In "All MIDI Inputs" enabled.

### Device Field (Windows Only)

The Device field in Figure 3.3 is unique to the Windows version of Cubase. There are two different types of MIDI devices in Windows: DirectMusic and Windows MIDI. DirectMusic devices are used by third-party MIDI hardware developers and will most likely be used by your MIDI interface. Windows MIDI devices are used to interface with components within the Windows operating system. For example, Figure 3.3 shows one Windows MIDI device to which is connected the Microsoft GS Wavetable Synth. This is a GS-compatible virtual synthesizer found in the Windows operating system. Without sounding too cruel, it's nothing to write home about. It can be used if you need to make GS-compatible SMF (Standard MIDI Files), but with the breadth of the Cubase sound palette, I doubt you'll ever need to use the Microsoft GS Wavetable Synth. To that end, I usually uncheck its visible box so that it doesn't create confusion.

### System Timestamp Settings (Windows Only)

The System Timestamp settings are a little hard to explain. The timing, or synchronization, of MIDI devices can be controlled either by Cubase or by Windows (System). By default, Cubase controls the timing; therefore, the System Timestamp checkboxes are disabled. However, if you need to have Windows control the timing, you'll need to enable the setting for the desired device (Windows MIDI and/ or DirectMusic.) Weirdly, every Windows-based PC will require either Cubase or Windows to control the timing.

But how do you know which timing method is best? There's only one way to find out, and that is by recording some MIDI information to the Cubase Click (Metronome) and then listening to the playback timing. If you find that the playback is ahead of the Click (as if you played way ahead of the beat, but you didn't), then you'll need to change the current System Timestamp setting. In other words, if the timing was noticeably off with System Timestamp disabled, you'll need to enable it, or vice versa.

If you don't know about the System Timestamp settings, the MIDI timing problem will be impossible to deduce. I've had customers spend hours or days trying to figure out why their MIDI tracks sound as if they were recorded in an alternate universe that exists several hundred milliseconds in the future. "I'll record quarter-notes on the beat of the metronome, but during playback, they're *ahead* of the beat," many a befuddled client has exclaimed. Hopefully by knowing about System Timestamp and how to change it, you'll save yourself the time and hassle.

# Configuring Your Audio Interface

Configuring the audio interface is very similar to configuring the MIDI interface. If you've already closed (or never opened) the Device Setup window, you can click on the Devices menu and select Device Setup.

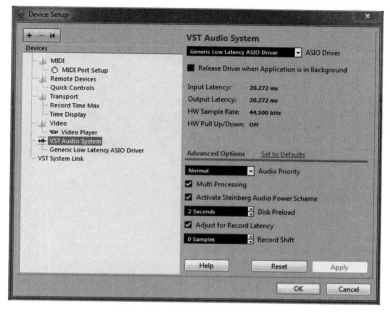

Figure 3.4: The VST Audio System window

On the left-hand side of the window (the Devices column), click on VST Audio System. On the right-hand side, find and click on the ASIO Driver drop-down selector. A list will appear from which you can select your audio interface. (Other interfaces, including the default Windows or Mac audio drivers, will appear in the list.) When you've selected your interface, a dialog box will appear asking you if you want to Switch or Keep the ASIO driver. Clicking on Switch will return you to the VST Audio System window.

## Changing Advanced Options

Usually the defaults (which you can always restore by clicking on Set to Defaults) will provide you with the proper Advanced Options settings. However, make sure that Multi Processing is enabled. That will allow Cubase to access all of the processors and cores of your computer's CPU. On a Windows computer, you'll also have the option to Activate Steinberg Audio Power Scheme. I would highly recommend enabling that option, because it will provide you with higher audio performance. Basically, Cubase will run your CPU to its rated performance and then restore the Windows Power Scheme after you quit Cubase. (Due to the nature of the OS, Mac users won't have to select a power scheme.)

## Interface-Specific Settings

Clicking on whatever appears directly underneath VST Audio System will allow you to further configure your audio interface. The reason I'm being so nonspecific in my directions is that your interface will determine the text; therefore, what's listed on your window will be different than mine.

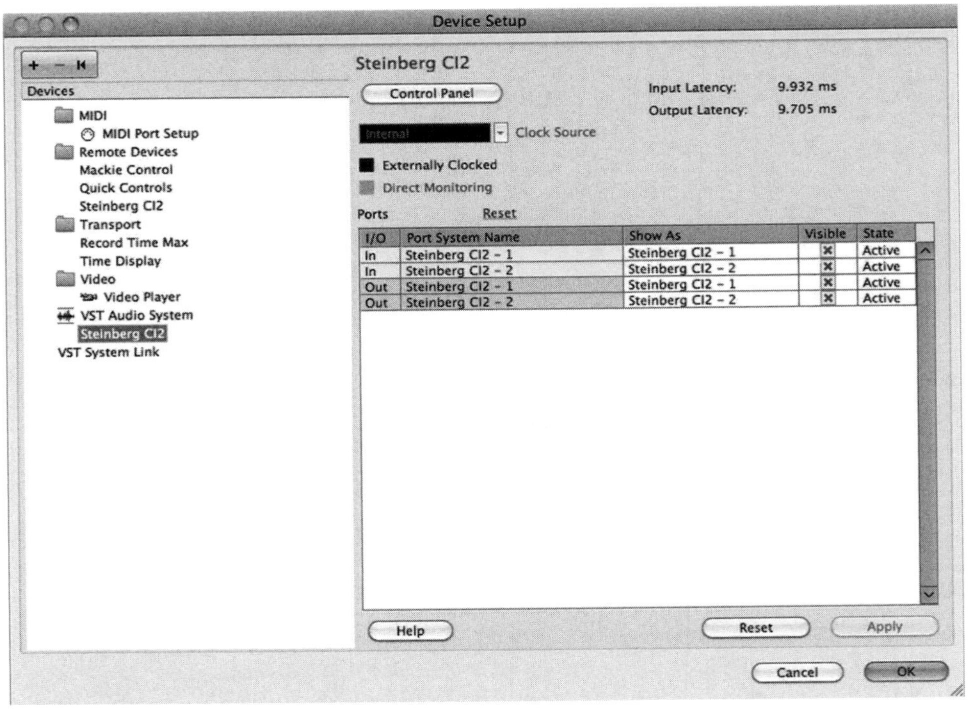

Figure 3.5: Interface-specific settings window

You'll notice that the text in Figure 3.5 says Steinberg CI2 directly beneath the VST Audio Settings. That's because I have a Steinberg CI2 audio interface. Your text, unless you happen to also use a CI2, will say something different. For example, if you're using a Presonus audio interface, then something like Presonus FP10 will be listed. Whatever the case may be, make sure to click on the name of your interface to change the following settings.

The In and Out port settings are very similar to the MIDI Port settings: yellow backgrounds are Ins, while blue backgrounds are Outs. The number of In and Out ports are determined by the physical connectors on your audio interface. For example, if your audio interface has sixteen inputs (like a Steinberg MR816CSX), then you'd see sixteen In ports and sixteen Out ports. In the case of my CI2 (in Figure 3.5), there are two of each: Input 1, Input 2, Output 1, and Output 2. (Another way to look at that would be Left Input, Right Input, Left Output, and Right Output.) Make sure that the visible checkboxes are enabled for any and all ports.

## Renaming the Audio Ports

If you'd like to rename the audio ports, you can double-click in the Show As field and type in a new name. This is useful for truncating a verbose name or for identifying a specific audio device (such as a microphone or drum machine) that is usually connected to an audio interface input. For example, in Figure 3.5, the name of the inputs are "Steinberg CI2–1" and "Steinberg CI2–2." I'd be tempted to change the names to "IN 1" and "IN 2." Or if I primarily recorded in stereo, then "IN Left" and "IN Right" would be appropriate. Finally, if I usually had my vocal mic plugged into the first input and my acoustic guitar pickup plugged into the second input, I could rename the ports "MIC" and "GTR." You could certainly just use the default port names, but being able to identify them more specifically is a nice feature.

## Control Panel Settings (Including Latency)

Clicking on the Control Panel button will reveal another window. However, the appearance of the window and the settings themselves will be specific to your audio interface. Therefore, I cannot speak about all the settings you might find on your control panel, save one: buffer size. The buffer size is what controls your audio interface latency. *Latency* is how long it takes for your computer to receive an audio signal at the interface In port and then send it to the interface Out port. Or in the case of virtual instruments, the buffer size determines how long it will take for MIDI information to be received, converted into audio by the virtual synthesizer, and then sent to the audio Out port. The faster your computer is, the lower the latency. However, there are many factors that can impact proper buffer size, including number of audio tracks, number of virtual instruments, number of notes being played on those virtual instruments, and number and type of effects processors (particularly reverb). Since all of those variables will impact the latency, the proper buffer size will be similarly variable.

The most common sign of a buffer set too low is popping and crackling in the audio playback. When the buffers are too low, the computer doesn't have enough room to sufficiently process the audio being produced by Cubase. If you hear popping and crackling or if you notice the VST Performance meter going into the red (see "VST Performance Meters," chapter 5), then you should increase the buffer size.

Conversely, a buffer set too high will result in longer latency times. In other words, you might hear some "lag" time between when you sing into the mic and you hear it in your headphones. Or in the case of MIDI tracks assigned to VST Instruments, you'll play a note on your MIDI controller, and the audio will come out of the speakers a few hundred milliseconds later (hence the term *latency*).

With all this in mind, the rule of thumb is to start your Cubase Projects with low buffer sizes. Then, as the number of Audio tracks, VST Instruments, and effects increase, so should the buffer sizes. A good rule of thumb is to start with buffer sizes between 128 and 384 samples, then increase the buffers to between 512 and 2,048 samples when you start mixing. Don't be afraid to make incremental adjustments throughout the development of each Cubase Project. Since the buffer size is systemic to Cubase, you can alter the size to fit the currently loaded project.

## Resetting Your Audio System

Cubase, like any computer program, can crash or become inoperative. So can your audio interface. That's why there's a Reset button located on the bottom of the window. (See Figure 3.5.) Clicking the Reset button will interrupt the audio processing and restart the Cubase audio engine. If you notice that your audio interface has become unresponsive, you may want to click the Reset button. If that doesn't reestablish the audio system, you'll need to save your work and restart Cubase. In the case of USB or FireWire audio interfaces, you may need to unplug them from the computer and their own power sources to fully reset them. Or if your audio interface is nonremovable (like a PCI or PCI Express card), you may need to shut down and unplug the computer for the audio interface to fully reset.

# The Negative Impact of Wi-Fi and Ethernet Controllers

I've mentioned that low buffer settings can induce popping, crackling, stuttering, and other anomalies into your recordings and playback. These are problems that can appear on any computer running any DAW program. There are other factors that can seriously degrade your computer's music-production capabilities. One of the most common causes is network traffic on Wi-Fi (Wireless Internet) and even hardware Ethernet network controllers. Some computers will not exhibit audio anomalies during network activity. However, if you've increased your buffer size and are still getting the occasional pop or click, you may want to disable your network controllers. (Note: Some of you cross-platform users can attest that Windows exhibits far more network-induced audio problems than Mac OS. However, I've seen this phenomenon on both platforms. Better safe than sorry.)

Network activity can occur even when you're not actively surfing the Internet or accessing another computer or server. Parts of the Mac OS, Windows, and other applications occasionally create network traffic. When they do, they can create pops, clicks, and stutters. Here's a good way to find out if your network controllers are causing such problems. Load a Cubase Project that contains Audio or VST Instrument tracks and start playback. Then load a web browser and start surfing to some websites. If you notice an increase in popping and clicking during the time a webpage is loading, you should disable your network controllers. Here's how to do it.

## Disabling Network Controllers on Vista and Windows 7

Click on your Start button, and then select Control Panel. Click on Network and Internet, and then click on Network and Sharing Center. On the left-hand side of the screen, click on Change adapter settings. Right-click on each and every connection, and select Disable. Usually the Local Area Connection(s) or Wireless Network Connection(s) is the culprit. Then return to Cubase to see if the pops and clicks are gone. When you're done making music and want to get the computer back on the Net, repeat the process, but click Enable.

## Disabling Network Controllers on Windows XP and Media Center Edition

Click on your Start button and select Control Panel, then double-click on Network Connections. Right-click on each and every connection and select Disable. Usually the Local Area Connection(s) or Wireless Network Connection(s) is the culprit. Then return to Cubase to see if the pops and clicks are gone. When you're done making music and want to get the computer back on the Net, repeat the process, but click Enable.

## Disabling Network Controllers on Mac OS X

If you're connected to a network via your AirPort card, you can simply click on the Airport icon in the upper right-hand side of your Finder menu bar and select Turn AirPort Off. However, if you're connected through the Ethernet port, it's a little more work. Click on the Apple button in the upper left-hand corner, and select System Preferences. Click on Network, and then click on the Ethernet port on the left-hand side of the window. Click on the Configure IPv4: drop-down menu, and select Off. You may want to do the same thing with the AirPort, FireWire, and any other device that appears on the left. Then return to Cubase to see if the pops and clicks are gone. When you're done making music and want to get the computer back on the Net, repeat the process, but click Enable.

# Getting Rid of Hum and Buzz

Before I go further, let me preface by saying that this procedure may be dangerous and could result in electric shock. Hum and buzz in audio systems (including computers) are usually caused by ground (earth) loops. The ground (you know, the Earth's dirty crust we walk on and grow food in) is part of the electrical circuit. Electricity needs a path to ground to be safe. If spurious charges are created within an electrical circuit, they'll start looking for the point of least resistance into which they'll harmlessly disperse. That point is the ground. If there is no path to ground, it will flow to the next point of least resistance, which could very well be the human body: *your* human body. These spurious charges could be a tiny shock, or they could carry enough amperage to injure or even kill you. Therefore, before you use a ground lifter (as I will describe in the next paragraph), understand the dangers.

## Using a Ground Lifter

That being said, ground loops are caused by having more than one path to ground. For example, if you plug a keyboard's audio outputs to your audio interface and there's suddenly an audible hum or buzz, chances are the keyboard has one path to ground and the computer has another path to ground. One or both devices would have to have a three-prong AC cable for this to occur. Using a ground lifter will remove the ground wire from a 3-prong power cable.

Figure 3.6: A ground lifter

Ground lifters are available at hardware stores or even the household section of your local market. You can connect a ground lifter to the power cable of either the keyboard or the computer to see if a ground loop is the cause of the hum. You'll still have one path to ground, but make sure to remove the ground lifter when you disconnect the audio cables from your interface. Otherwise, you may be removing both the audio pathway *and* your safe path to ground.

Checking for ground loops is even easier on laptops, because they have their own batteries. You can simply unplug the AC adapter from the laptop, even when the computer is running, to see if the hum goes away. If it does, try the ground lifter on the laptop's AC adapter. But just like with a desktop computer, remove the ground lifter after you've disconnected the audio device from the audio interface to reestablish a safe path to ground.

## Determining if Your Home or Studio Is Properly Wired

Using a ground lifter will serve no purpose if the AC outlet itself is not wired properly. Not only that, but improper electrical wiring can negatively impact the clarity of your audio pathway. I would recommend getting a wiring checker.

Figure 3.7: A wiring checker

While you're at the hardware store purchasing some ground lifters, grab a wiring checker. All you have to do is plug it into an electrical outlet to see if the sockets are wired properly. Dealing with all sorts of weird noises after moving my home studio to a new house, I went around and checked the wiring. My house was obviously wired on a Friday at about 4:30 p.m. Wires were reversed, and ground wires were rarely even connected. So not only did I have audio problems, there was also a significant risk of electrocution. If you determine that you have improperly wired plugs and you don't know your way around a fuse box, then hire a competent, bonded, and insured electrician to do it for you. Then, when he or she is finished, don't hesitate to double-check his or her work with your wiring checker (again, better safe than sorry).

## Use High-Quality Cables

If you've purchased Cubase, a great audio interface, and recording microphones, why would you ever want to connect them with cheap cables? Here's the rule: you may never hear the highest-quality component in your studio, but you'll always hear the lowest-quality component. More often than not, crappy cables cause bad audio, and you will hear them as they degrade or ruin your recordings. Do yourself a favor, and invest in some good cables with ample shielding. Your local music-store salesperson can lead you to the good stuff.

# The Project Assistant Window

The Project Assistant window usually appears immediately after you launch Cubase. However, we had to close the window to facilitate the setup of the audio and MIDI interfaces. To reopen the Project Assistant, click on the File menu and select New Project.

## Definition of a Cubase Project

Before we dive into the Project Assistant too deeply, let's discuss what a Cubase Project is. A project is simply the document you'll be using in Cubase. But why isn't it called a song or a tune or a composition? Because those names wouldn't work for sound-effects designers, special-event recordings, or any of the other unique purposes Cubase can facilitate. It's the same reason a word processor doesn't refer to its documents as novels, poems, or lesson plans. *Project* is simply more generic. So whenever you're about to create music (or any other sound-related undertaking) with Cubase, it will be called a project.

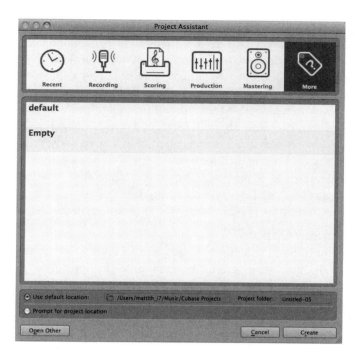

Figure 3.8: The Project Assistant window

## Cubase Templates

The Project Assistant comes with a wide variety of Cubase templates. *Templates* are projects with preassembled tracks and other settings that can make it easier to create a project. For example, at the top of the Project Assistant (see Figure 3.7) are six tabs: Recent, Recording, Scoring, Production, Mastering, and More. The latter is where you can store your own custom templates. It's a good idea to look at some of the templates that come with Cubase. But for now, click on the More tab and single-click on the Empty template.

The reason we're going to start with the Empty template is so that you can add and understand the types of tracks that we'll be adding. It will also allow you to more easily see the Project window in which you'll be spending a lot of time. Now before you're tempted to click the Create button, it is critical that we understand media management.

## Cubasic #1: Using Proper Media Management

If you learn only one thing while reading this book, I hope you commit to using proper media management. If you don't, you're setting yourself up for a lot of unnecessary work and hassle. Cubase, like all DAW software, creates a large number of files on your computer. Every time you hit the Record button on an Audio track, it creates a new audio file on your hard disk that is separate from the Cubase Project file. Unless you define the Project Folder in which to store those audio files, they'll be stored at unpredictable locations.

They might also be stored in one central folder, which would make it impossible to determine which audio files belong to which projects. This can make it impossible to accurately archive a project when it's completed. For example, I recently visited a very prolific composer who needed me to archive some of his work onto a separate hard drive. (Archiving, or backing up your projects, is of paramount importance.) But he stored all of his projects into one folder. Finding the Project files was easy enough (there were about one hundred), but there were over two hundred thousand audio files! Can you imagine trying to figure out which of the files went with which project? Even the naming of the audio files didn't help. Of the two hundred thousand-plus audio files, 68,776 had the word *vocal* in the file name. He was in for a long and expensive night.

Fortunately, Cubase has a way to reassemble the Cubase Project and its audio files into a new Project Folder. However, it's quite labor intensive, and it will only get in the way of your workflow. If you use proper media management, you'll never have to go through this hassle or pay me by the hour to do it for you.

(Note: The procedure I'm about to show may seem very involved the first time you do it. However, after a little practice, you'll be able to do it in less than five seconds. Five seconds now can save you five hours later.)

### The Two Media-Management Options
Cubase offers two different options for media management: Default location and Prompt for project location. Both of those options are located at the bottom of the Project Assistant window.

We won't be using the Default location option, because I really want to illustrate how media management works. However, if you already have a grasp of media management and wish to use that Default location option, make sure you set the Default location and create a newly named Project Folder for this and every project. (See Figure 3.9.)

We are going to use the Prompt for project location option. Click on the Radio button to the left of Prompt for project location. You'll notice that the Create button turns into a Continue button. Go ahead and click Continue.

Figure 3.9: The two media-management options

### The Set Project Folder Window
The next window to appear will differ slightly between the Windows and Mac versions. However, the function is the same: to choose the location for the Project Folder on your computer. I will show you both, but I'll also be showing two common places for your Project Folder. So make sure you read both the Windows and Mac instructions that follow.

The first popular location is your Music folder inside your user folder. In the case of Figure 3.10, it's located at my user name (Matt_I715w7) and then in the My Music folder. To set a Project Folder here, I would recommend clicking the New Folder button and creating a folder called "Cubase Projects." (You'll only have to do that this one time. Then every other project you create can then be stored in the Cubase Projects folder.) Inside that folder, create a folder called "My First Cubase Project," then click OK.

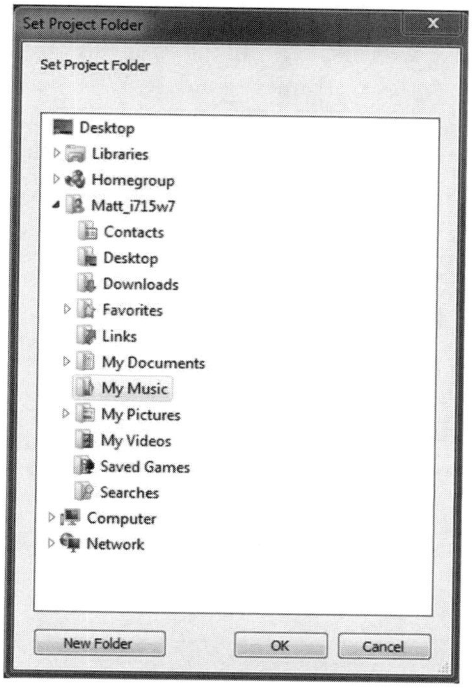

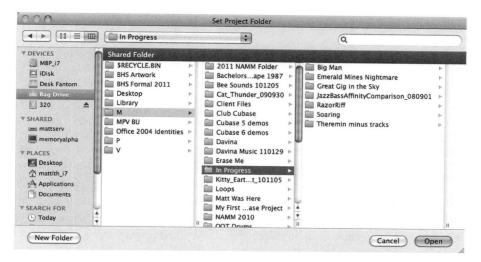

Figure 3.10: Set Project Folder/Windows 7/User Music Folder

If you're a power user like me, you may have already installed an additional hard disk into your computer to store your Cubase projects. In my case, it's an external eSATA hard disk attached to my MacBook Pro (which requires an ExpressCard3/4 eSATA card). I highly recommend using an additional hard disk for Cubase Project storage. You'll get more performance and more room, plus you won't lose your work if your system hard disk fails. To that end, I've selected (see Figure 3.11) my external hard disk (Bag Drive), then selected the M folder (short for music) and the In Progress folder (where I store my music rather than my client's music). From there, click the New Folder button and title the new folder "My First Cubase Project." When finished, click the Open button.

Figure 3.11: Set Project Folder/Mac OS X/Eternal Hard Disk

## Saving the Project File into the Project Folder

After you've set the Project Folder, Cubase will display a blank project named "Untitled1." The window that is displayed is called the Project window. We'll learn more about that later. Right now, we need to complete the last step in accomplishing proper media management: saving the Project file into the Project Folder you just created. Click on the File menu and select Save As.

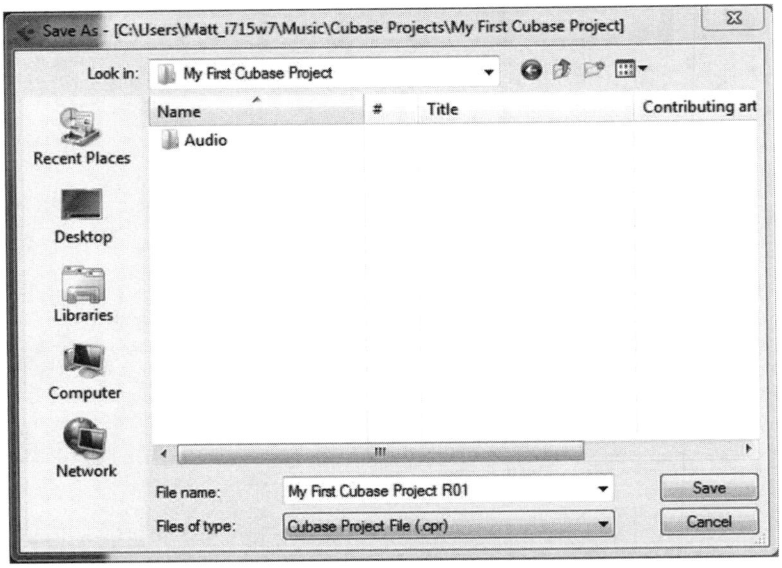

Figure 3.12: The Save As window/Windows 7

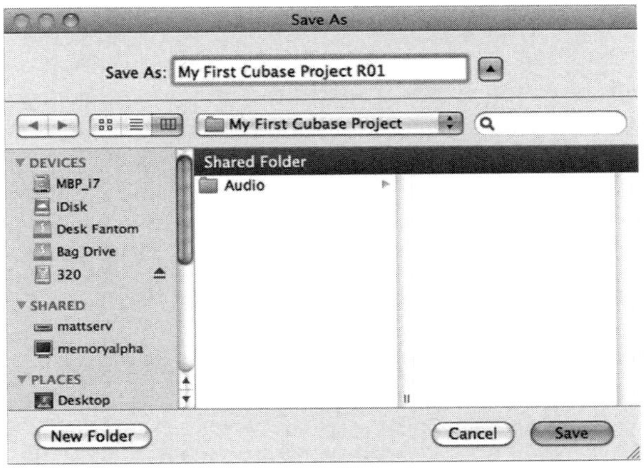

Figure 3.13: The Save As window/Mac OS X

The Save As window will differ slightly between Windows and Mac; however, the function is the same: to save the Project file into the Project Folder. You'll notice that in either case, the Project Folder gets selected as the storage location automatically. This way, you'll never have to navigate to the location of the Project Folder (another benefit of using proper media management). All you have to do is type in the desired name of the Project file. That name should be the same name as the Project Folder. In this case, type, "My First Project File R01." (More on the "R01" in a moment.) You'll also notice in Figure 3.12 that "Cubase Project File (.cpr)" is selected. While both Windows and Macs use file extensions, only the Windows version gives you the option to change it. So regardless of which version you use, don't worry about including ".cpr" in the file name, because it's done automatically. When you have the Project file named, click the Save button to return to the Project window.

## Understanding the Benefits of Proper Media Management

The biggest advantages of proper media management are focus and portability. Let's talk about focus first. In Figures 3.12 and 3.13, you'll notice the Audio Folder that Cubase automatically created when you made the Project Folder. From now on, when you're working on the "My First Cubase Project R01" project, the audio files will get stored in the corresponding audio Folder. In other words, Cubase focuses on that audio Folder and stores every audio file within it. In fact, as you get further along on a project, you'll notice other items automatically created by Cubase and stored in the Project Folder. These will include the Images Folder (graphic depictions of the audio waveforms), Edits Folder (processed audio files), Freeze Folder (offline frozen audio files), Video Folder (video files) and .bak (backup) files.

Cubase is focused on the Project Folder while you're working on the Project file. That means that every piece of media that was created by you or Cubase will be stored in the Project Folder. That makes your Cubase Project very portable. Portability is critical, but not limited to, the following situations:

- Moving a project from one hard disk to another.
- Backing up a project to another hard disk or DVD data disc.
- Moving a project between two or more computers.
- Sharing projects between different people with different computers.

In any case, when you use proper media management, all you have to do is move, back up, or share the Project Folder, because it contains all of the elements of the project.

Now just in case I haven't properly motivated you to use proper media management, I charge $600 per day, plus expenses and travel costs, and would love to fly to your studio to clean up your Cubase (or any other DAW) media problems. With an ominous-sounding voice comically drenched in reverb, I say unto you, "You've been warned!"

## Using Matt's Project-Revision-Naming Method

In Figure 3.12 and 3.13, you'll notice that I added "R01" at the end of the Project file name. To me, that indicates the first version of a project. Then when I'm about to significantly add to or edit a project, I'll perform a Save As command with an incremental version number. In other words, R01 would have all the tracks created and named. R02 would include the drum tracking. R03 would include the bass guitar tracking, R04 the guitars, R05 the vocals, and so on. That way, I can always go back to a previous version (which I call "swimming upstream") if the need arises.

I use that same method when I'm mastering a project. In other words, "My First Cubase Project R10M07" would be the seventh version of mastering on the tenth version of the project or "mix." That way I always know which version of a project I'm mastering, and I can return to that project if it needs any tweaking that was revealed in the mastering stage.

# Enabling Auto Save

Have you ever worked really hard on a word processor document, email, or other computer-related project only to have it disappear due to a crash, power failure, or accidentally hitting Don't Save before closing the program? It's happened to me, it's happened to you, and it happens to everyone who uses a computer. We all know we're supposed to occasionally save the file while we're working on it. However, we creative types tend to neglect that practice when the music is flowing. To help spare you from such an unfortunate occurrence, Cubase has an Auto Save feature that will execute the Save command for you at regular intervals.

Auto Save is located in the Cubase Preferences window. On Windows, go to the File menu and select Preferences. On Mac, go to the Cubase menu and select Preferences.

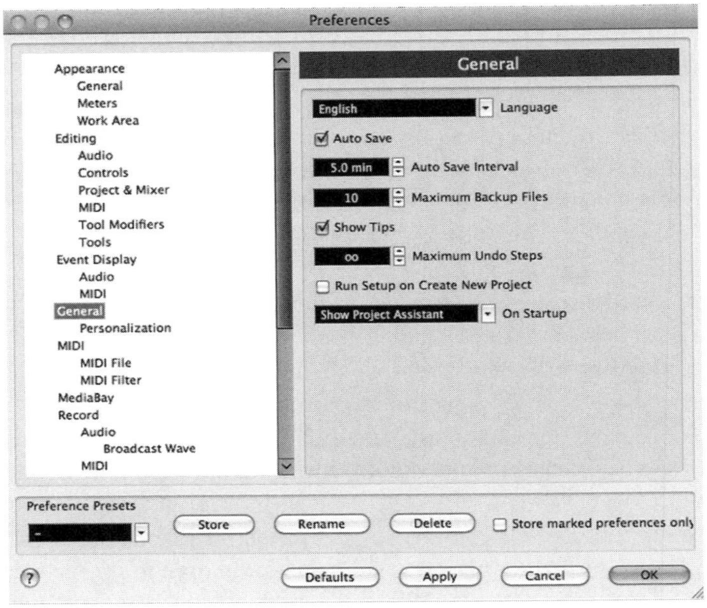

Figure 3.14: The Preferences window

The Preferences window is divided into left and right halves. The left side contains the preferences, while the right side shows the settings for the selected preference. Click on the General preference and then observe the settings on the right. I usually find that Auto Save is enabled on default. However, due to the importance of this preference, now is a great time to make sure that Auto Save is enabled. The Interval is definable. I usually set it to 5.0 seconds. However, if you're working with a large number of tracks or VST Instruments that use a lot of samples (such as Steinberg HALion 4, The Grand, or Native Instruments Kontakt), you'll notice that the process of saving takes longer. Therefore, you may want to set the Interval to 10.0 or 15.0 minutes.

Every time Cubase Auto Saves the project, it will make a backup file. As I mentioned previously, backup files have a .bak rather than a .cpr file and are saved in the Project Folder. The default Maximum Backup Files setting is 10, but you can set this as you see fit. When you've set the Preferences appropriately, you can click Apply and/or OK at the bottom of the Preferences window.

# I/O, I/O, It's Off to Work You'll Go

We're very close to being able to start recording our first tracks. However, we still need to configure your hardware Ins and Outs. We'll do that in the next chapter.

# Chapter 4

# THE INS AND OUTS OF CUBASE . . . LITERALLY

**A** computer is an input/output device. In other words, you put stuff in, and you get stuff out. For example, you put text into a word processor, and you get a printed page out of your printer. You input a search into Google, and you'll see the output of results. Or in the case of a compelling computer game, you put in every waking minute, and what you get out is another dateless night. I hope you're not currently deeply involved in any computer games, because we have a lot of music to get into and out of Cubase. In this chapter, you will learn about:

- Assigning MIDI inputs and outputs.
- Configuring your audio inputs and outputs.
- Creating a simple Control Room (Cubase only).
- When to record in mono, stereo, or multichannel.
- Setting the Metronome (Click).
- Recording some test tracks to confirm your software and hardware configuration.

## Cubasic #2: Assigning MIDI Inputs and Outputs to Tracks

In chapter 3, we learned how to configure your MIDI interface. Now I'll show you how to assign those MIDI inputs and outputs to MIDI and Instrument tracks. Before proceeding, make sure you have your "My First Cubase Project" project loaded. What you should be seeing is a blank Project window.

Window Layout Button

Figure 4.1: A blank Project window

We'll learn more about the Project window in the next chapter. For now, what you're looking at are the three columns of the Project window: Inspector, Track List, and Event Display. If you're only seeing two columns, it's because the Inspector is currently disabled. To enable the Inspector, click on the Window Layout button (see Figure 4.1, second toolbar button from the left), and make sure Inspector has a check next to it. To close the Window Layout screen, you can either wait for a few seconds or click anywhere outside the Window Layout screen boundary.

## Creating a MIDI Track

Now you'll need to add one MIDI track so that I can show you how the MIDI inputs and outputs work. Click on the Project menu, select Add Track, and then select MIDI. The Add MIDI Track dialog box will appear, but all you need to do is make sure the count is set to "1," and then hit Add Track in the lower right-hand corner.

Notice that the MIDI track has been given the arbitrary name of MIDI 01.

Figure 4.2: 1 MIDI track added to project

## Assigning MIDI Input, Output, and Channel

Now that we've added the track, we can assign its MIDI Input, Output, and Channel. Every MIDI or Instrument track has all three of those assignable parameters.

The Inspector has several sections in a vertical order. The topmost section is usually colorized and contains the name of the track. The MIDI assignments are located underneath the top section. If you can't see the settings listed in Figure 4.2 (the Track MIDI settings), you may need to click on the top section to reveal the settings.

## Track MIDI Input

Near the center of the top section, you will find the Track MIDI Input setting. Currently it's assigned to All MIDI Inputs. That means that the MIDI track can receive and record MIDI information from any In port in the MIDI Port Setup window. (See "The MIDI Port Setup Settings," chapter 3.) If you'd like to choose a specific In port, you can click on the All MIDI Inputs setting, which will reveal a list of all the available In ports. Make sure it's not set to Not Connected, or you won't be able to record MIDI information onto that track.

Another way to think about the Track MIDI Input is to ask the question, "Where do I want the MIDI information to be received from?" It could be your USB MIDI keyboard, your pad controller, or a device connected to a MIDI interface port.

## Track MIDI Output

Similarly to the Input setting, the Track MIDI Output setting will allow you to route the MIDI or Instrument track to the desired Out port destination. In Figure 4.2, it's assigned to Network Session 1. Clicking on that setting will reveal a list of all the available destinations.

Figure 4.3: Track MIDI Output destinations

In Figure 4.3, I've reassigned the destination of Track MIDI 01 from Network Session 1 to Taurus-3 Bass Pedal, which is an external synthesizer with its own USB port for MIDI. (I guess I'd better call the neighbors and prepare them for the onslaught of rumbling bass frequencies they'll experience when I play them.)

Another way to think about the Track MIDI Output is to ask the question, "Where do I want the MIDI information to be sent to?" Again, it could be any device that appears in your MIDI Port Setup window (see "The MIDI Port Setup Settings," chapter 3), or it could also be a VST Instrument inside Cubase. We'll discuss that possibility later.

## Track MIDI Channel

Every MIDI device can receive on any one of sixteen MIDI channels. Some devices can receive MIDI information on multiple channels including all sixteen simultaneously. Setting the Track MIDI Channel allows you to assign the track to the desired device. If you refer back to Figure 4.2, you'll see that the channel of the MIDI 01 track is set to 1. Clicking on that setting will drop down a list of the sixteen MIDI channels, including a special Any setting that allows the MIDI channel of the event itself (that's recorded on the track) to determine the MIDI channelization. Chances are you won't use that setting very often, if at all. But do make sure to set the MIDI channel to the same channel number as the MIDI device to which you'll be sending the MIDI information.

Note: There are sixteen MIDI channels that can travel through one MIDI port. This allows you to "daisy-chain" MIDI cables from one device to another. Setting the MIDI channel of both the track and the MIDI device will establish proper MIDI communication. This is true of both hardware and software MIDI devices. While setting the MIDI channel is an important step, there are times when you won't have to assign the channel. This situation usually occurs when using VST Instruments or virtual instruments from within Cubase. When that situation arises later in this book, I'll let you know. We won't be able to discuss all the principles of MIDI. So if you'd like to learn more, I'd recommend reading Jeff Rona's *The MIDI Companion* from Hal Leonard.

## MIDI Settings Are Made Track by Track

It's important to note that every MIDI or Instrument track has its own MIDI settings. That means that you'll need to verify the settings for every track. If you don't, erroneous settings can result in frustrating communication problems.

# Cubasic #3: Configuring Your VST Connections

The inputs and outputs of your audio hardware must be configured to the inputs and outputs of Cubase. These routings are known as VST Connections. To access the VST Connections window, click the Devices menu and select VST Connections, or type F4 on your computer keyboard. (For Mac users, see "'F' or Function Keys," chapter 2.)

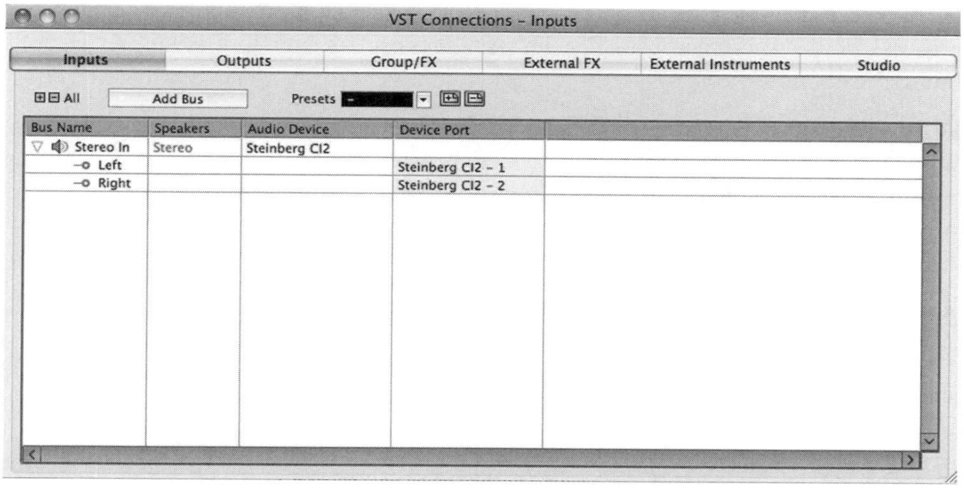

Figure 4.4: The VST Connections window/Inputs tab

## Assigning Audio Inputs to Cubase

There are two (Cubase Artist and Elements) or six (Cubase) tabs at the top of the VST Connections window. To configure the inputs, make sure you click on the Inputs tab. Then click on the Presets drop-down box and select the 1 x Stereo preset. (Note: We will only be configuring one stereo input at this time. In a later chapter, we'll discuss adding the additional audio inputs on your audio interface, if applicable.)

Now your VST Connections window will look very similar to Figure 4.4. In the Bus Name column, you'll see one bus named Stereo In. If you don't see the left and right ports directly beneath the Bus Name, click the little triangle to the left of Stereo In.

Now look across to the Audio Device column. If Not Connected is listed, click on it to reveal your audio interface. In my case, it's my Steinberg CI2 interface. Then in the Device Port column, if Not Connected is listed, click on it to reveal the input ports of your audio interface. In my case, the left bus is connected to Steinberg CI2–1, and the right bus is connected to Steinberg CI2–2. Basically, the left bus is assigned to the first input of my audio interface, and the right bus is assigned to the second input of my audio interface. Your interface may designate the first input as 1, left, or A, while the second input could be 2, right, or B. Every audio interface manufacturer has its own preference for input designation, but just get the first input to the left bus and the second input to the right bus.

### Renaming an Input Bus

You can rename an input bus simply by single-clicking the current bus name, pausing for a second or two, then single-clicking the name again. The current name will become highlighted, and you can type in the desired name. In the case of Figure 4.4, I could name it "CI2 INs." Renaming the input buses is especially useful when your audio interface has more than two inputs.

### Storing an Input Preset

VST Connections are stored as part of each project. That means that different projects can have different VST Connection configurations. It's a very flexible system, but can get a little unwieldy when you use multiple VST Connections between a number of different projects. Fortunately, there is a Store button to the right of the Presets drop-down box. When you click on Store, you'll be given a dialog box in which to name the preset. I would recommend storing the current preset as something like "My Default Inputs."

### Why a Stereo Bus Instead of Two Mono Buses?

While there are occasions when mono buses are advantageous, Cubase allows you to assign mono tracks to either left or right input buses. Therefore, mono tracks can be addressed by either left or right buses. Conversely, stereo tracks must be addressed by stereo buses.

## Assigning Audio Outputs to Cubase

The process for assigning outputs is almost identical to that of inputs. Click on the Outputs tab at the top of the VST Connections window.

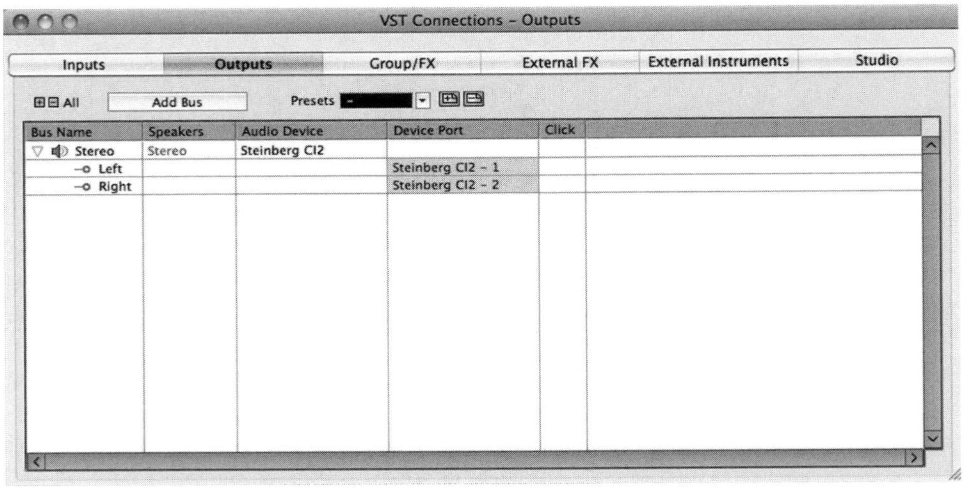

Figure 4.5: The VST Connections window/Outputs tab

Click on the Presets drop-down box and select the 1 x Stereo preset. You'll see one stereo output bus with left and right outputs. Make sure your audio interface is assigned in the Audio Device column. You should also check the Device Port column to make sure the left and right outputs are assigned to the left and right buses.

The procedures for renaming output buses and presets are identical to those for renaming the inputs. Also be aware that different Cubase Projects can use different output configurations, so make sure you store the outputs as something like "My Default Outputs."

## Special Considerations for the Cubase Outputs Settings

The output assignments accomplish two things: they direct the signal flow of Cubase to your audio interface hardware outputs, and they assign the Cubase Mixer Master Fader to the virtual output of Cubase. The latter is significant, because the Master Fader controls the volume level of your mixdowns and therefore the overall volume of the MP3s and audio CDs you'll be creating. It's very important not to use the Master Fader (on the Mixer) of Cubase to control your monitor speaker volume, because it will impact the volume level of your mixdown. It's better to use the physical volume control on the audio interface or create a Control Room with which to adjust monitor level.

# Creating a Simple Control Room (Cubase Only)

The Control Room is a fantastic feature of Cubase. It allows you to assign the inputs and outputs of your audio hardware to common destinations, such as monitor speakers, headphone mixes, and talkback microphones. The advantages of the Control Room become very significant when your audio interface has more than two inputs or two outputs. However, there is one specific advantage you'll enjoy by creating even the simplest of Control Rooms: independent volume controls for the mixdown and the studio monitor volume from within Cubase.

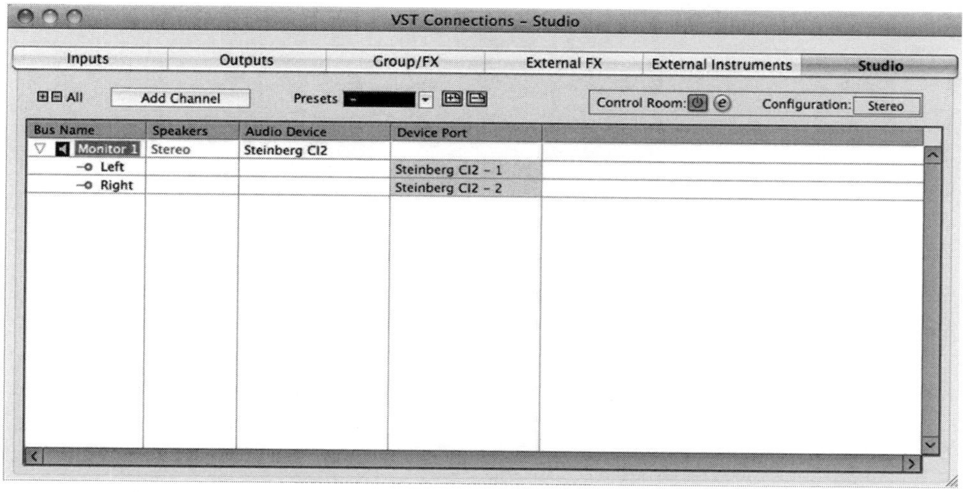

Figure 4.6: The VST Connections window/Studio tab

To configure your Control Room, click on the Studio tab at the top of the VST Connections window.

## Enabling the Control Room

If this is the first time you've gone to the Studio tab, chances are good that the Control Room is turned off. Click on the Control Room power button, and turn it on. You'll see a notification screen saying that the Control Room is indeed disabled and asking if you'd like to enable it. Click on Enable. You'll see a new bus added to the Bus Name column called Monitor 1, and it will have a left and right output channel. You might also have the Control Room Mixer displayed after turning on the Control Room power. If that's the case, close the Control Room Mixer for now. Your Studio tab should now look like Figure 4.6.

Monitor 1 is the destination for your studio monitors. If you have an audio interface with more than two outputs and you have more than one pair of studio monitors, you can create as many as four monitors, and the Cubase Control Room will allow you to switch between all of them. But for now, all you need to do is connect the hardware outputs of your audio interface to the inputs of your monitor speakers.

### Assigning the Audio Device and Device Ports to the Control Room

Assigning the Audio Device and Device Ports settings to the Monitor 1 bus is identical to the procedure for assigning outputs in the Outputs tab. All you need to do is assign your audio interface to the Audio Device column, and then assign the left bus to the left Device Port and the right bus to the right Device Port.

The procedures for renaming Control Room buses and presets are identical to those of the inputs and outputs. And just like inputs and outputs, different Cubase Projects can use different Control Room configurations. Therefore, make sure you store the Control Room preset as something like "My Control Room."

### A Funny Thing Happened on the Way to the Control Room

By assigning your audio interface left and right ports to the Monitor 1 bus, you've also disconnected them from the Outputs tab. Click on the Outputs tab at the top of the VST Connections window to see what I'm talking about.

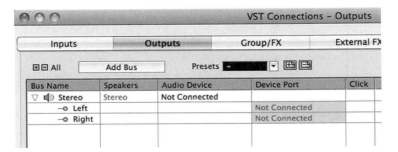

Figure 4.7: Outputs bus disconnected

After taking the time to make the proper assignments in the Outputs tab, you may be a little miffed that the Control Room has automatically disconnected the Audio Device and Device Ports. However, this is normal. By doing so, the Cubase Master Fader is now in full control of the mixdown volume only, while the Control Room volume (i.e., your studio monitors) can be adjusted without impacting the volume of the mixdown.

I should mention that it's not critical to use the Control Room. But I think after you've experienced even the most minor of its advantages, you'll enjoy using the Control Room for all of your monitoring needs.

# Assigning Audio Inputs and Outputs to Audio Tracks

Now that you've made the proper input and output settings in the VST Connections window, you'll need to know how to assign them to Audio tracks. To that end, we'll need to add some Audio tracks to our project. Make sure you have your "My First Cubase Project" project loaded, then click on the Project menu and select Add Track, and then click on Audio. The Add Audio Track dialog box will appear, on which you can set the Count to "1" and the Configuration to Stereo. Click the Add Track button in the lower right-hand corner of the Add Audio Track dialog box. Now repeat the process, but this time, set the Track Configuration to Mono.

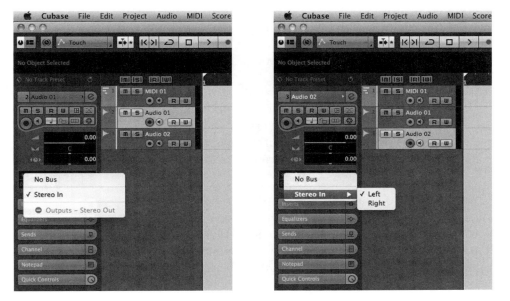

Figure 4.8: Audio tracks added to the Cubase Project

You'll find the two new Audio tracks added underneath the MIDI track you created earlier. The Audio tracks will have the default names of Audio 01 and Audio 02, respectively. We can now assign audio inputs to those tracks.

## Assigning Audio Inputs to Stereo and Mono Tracks

Stereo tracks can only be addressed from Stereo buses, while Mono tracks can be addressed from either Mono or Stereo buses. Look at Figure 4.8, and locate the Track Audio Input setting. Click on that setting, then take a close look at the following figure:

Figure 4.9: Track Audio Inputs on Stereo vs. Mono Audio tracks

Figure 4.9 is divided to show the different Track Audio Input settings for a Stereo Audio track (Audio 01) and a Mono Audio track (Audio 02). Notice that the Stereo Track Audio Input can only be assigned to Stereo In (as defined in the VST Connections Input tab). However, the Mono Track Audio Input can be assigned to either the left or right input of the Stereo In. This is why I usually create Stereo buses in the VST Connections Input tab. However, if you'd rather have Mono buses, don't let me stop you. In fact, Cubase will allow you to create Mono and Stereo buses that are assigned to the same Audio Device and Device Ports. (Cubase is a flexible little minx, indeed.)

## Assigning Tracks to Audio Outputs

If you refer back to Figure 4.8, you'll find the Track Audio Output settings. Most of the time, Audio tracks are assigned to the Stereo Out bus as defined on the Outputs tab of the VST Connections window. That means that you won't have to worry about changing this setting unless you have specific need to do so. Such occasions usually include assigning a number of Audio tracks to a Group Channel track or when routing Cubase tracks directly to independent audio interface hardware outputs. The latter is only necessary when interconnecting your audio interface to another audio device that has multiple inputs, such as a mixer or the audio interface of another computer. The bottom line is that unless you encounter such a specific need, leave the Track Audio Output set to the Stereo Out bus. (If you changed the name of the Stereo Out bus in the Output tab of the VST Connections window, make sure the Track Audio Output is set to that bus. Otherwise, you won't be able to hear the playback from the Audio track.)

Before proceeding, go ahead and save your Cubase Project by clicking on the File menu and selecting Save.

# When to Record in Mono, Stereo, or Multichannel

When people start recording their first Audio tracks, there can be some confusion as to whether to record in mono or stereo. A lot of that confusion comes from hearing other seasoned audio engineers say things like, "Stereo sounds better," or "Mono recordings are from the 1950s." Therefore, we should always record in stereo, right?

Well, the answer isn't quite that simple. The contemporary recording practices usually involve recording in one of three input configurations: mono, stereo, or multichannel. But how do you know which one is right for the recording you're about to make? I've found a way to easily determine the answer.

## Count Your Sources

Sources, in this case, would be the origin of the audio device or signal you want to record. Some signals are mono, while others are stereo. Multichannel signals will require a mix of mono and/or stereo input configurations. All you need to do is count the sources to determine the proper input configuration. To help you further understand this concept, let's take a look at some examples.

### Common Mono Sources

A single microphone is the most common mono source. A microphone (unless it's a specialized stereo microphone) has one output. One output equals one source. So when you're recording a vocalist, acoustic guitar, or trumpet with one microphone, the input configuration needs to be set to mono. Other mono sources might include a synthesizer with a single audio output or a bass guitar connected directly to the audio interface.

Creating a mono Audio track would be required to accurately record any of these examples.

### Are Vocals Stereo?

The human voice is not inherently stereo. The vocal cords, while they consist of a pair, can emit only one sound, or one source. Vocals only become stereo when they're recorded onto a mono track and then processed with some sort of stereo treatment. In an acoustic environment—for example, the live performance of an opera—the sound of the performer's voice as it bounces around the opera house creates a stereo image. That image can be created in Cubase by using a reverb processor such as the REVerence. Other stereo treatments of mono Audio tracks include panning the track further to the left or right side of the Stereo Out. Each track has its own pan (short for panorama) control to place a track at a specific location within the stereo mix. The bottom line is that while vocalists are not stereophonic, you can use panning and effect treatments to give them a sense of stereo.

### Common Stereo Sources

Most electronic musical instruments have a stereo output. In other words, they have one output connection labeled Left (or L) and another output connection labeled Right (or R). These include synthesizers, drum machines, samplers, phonographs, and CD players. When capturing the sound from a device that has stereo outputs, you should create a stereo Audio track upon which to record.

But stereo recording is not limited to electronic devices. Many acoustic instruments are inherently stereo. For example, when you're sitting at a grand piano and you play some low notes, the sound will be louder in your left ear than in your right. Playing middle C results in the sound being heard equally in both ears. Notes above middle C will be louder in the right ear than the left. And the higher the note, the more dramatically the sound will be sensed by your right ear. Therefore, to accurately record a grand piano, you should use at least two microphones in a stereo configuration. In other words, one mic pointed at the low strings and another pointed at the high strings. When you count the sources, you end up with two. Therefore, you should create and record on a stereo Audio track.

Many acoustic instruments are more accurately recorded with two microphones in a stereo configuration. That's because the sonic characteristics of the instrument are measurably different from the right and left "halves" of the instrument. These include, but are not limited to, an acoustic guitar, harp, vibraphone, string quartet, or vocal choir.

### Common Multichannel Sources

Perhaps the most demonstrative of multichannel examples is the recording of a drum set. In the early days of pop music, a drum set was recorded using only one microphone. However, the contemporary practice would be to put a microphone on every instrument that makes up a drum set and then record each microphone onto its own mono Audio track.

If we take a look at a five-piece drum set, it consists of a bass (or kick) drum, snare drum, two rack toms, one floor tom, one hi-hat cymbal, plus a multitude of other cymbals. To accurately record the essence of the entire drum set, you'd need at least eight microphones and an audio interface with eight discrete inputs, such as the Steinberg MR816CSX. (See "Choosing an Audio Interface," chapter 2.) Then you'd create eight mono Audio tracks to capture each component of the drum set. Usually they'd be kick, snare, hi-hat, tom 1, tom 2, floor tom, overhead left, and overhead right. The overhead microphones are placed above the drum set to capture not only the ride, crash and other cymbals, but also the ambient stereophonic essence of the whole drum set.

Figure 4.10: Drummer/engineer extraordinaire Tony Korologos sitting behind a properly miked five-piece drum set (not pictured: bass drum mic)
*Photo courtesy of Tony Korologos*

Then, prior to or immediately after the recording, the drum tracks would be panned according to their placement in the stereo image of the listener. In other words, the hi-hat track would be panned toward the listener's right ear while the floor tom would be panned toward the listener's left ear. Usually the overhead microphones are recorded onto their own separate mono Audio track so that panning and EQ (tone controls) can be applied independently. When I record a five-piece drum set, I'll usually mic the snare drum with two microphones: one over the top head and one underneath the bottom head. The same is true of the bass drum: one on each side of the drum to capture the front and rear heads separately. Also, make sure to have some 3-in-1 household oil for lubricating the bass drum pedal. Otherwise, you may be capturing the squeak of a poorly maintained bass drum pedal. (Listen to any of the early James Brown recordings such as "Get Up" or "I Feel Good," or Led Zeppelin recordings [especially "Bonzo's Montreux" from the *Coda* album], for examples of squeaky bass drum pedals.) Basically, the more microphones you record with, the more options you'll have during the mix.

The same is true for any large instrument or ensemble. For example, a large vocal ensemble such as the Mormon Tabernacle Choir would need a lot of microphones on each section (bass, tenor, alto, and soprano) to accurately record the performance. Care would also need to be exercised for capturing the pipe organ, piano, or any other accompanying instrumentation onto their own tracks. Then recording each microphone onto its own Audio track (mono or stereo, depending on the microphone placement) would allow for discrete volume, pan, EQ settings, and other treatments to be applied during the mix.

# Cubasic #4: Configuring and Recording with the Click or Metronome

For many years, music has been recorded while the performers listened to a metronome or click track in their headphones. This allowed for a noticeably tighter "feel" of the recording, because all the musicians were aware of the true tempo. Every DAW, including Cubase, has a Metronome with which you can accomplish the same tight feel.

Note: Cubase uses the terms Click, Clik, and Metronome interchangeably.

Not only are the recordings tighter, but the Metronome also establishes an accurate time base within Cubase. While there are many different time bases to choose from, the default of measures, bars, beats, and clocks is the most common and useful. That way, when the artist says, "Let's pick it up from measure 57," you'll know right where to go.

## Reluctance to Use the Metronome

The members of a band are used to playing their instruments together at the same time. But their "vibe" can be seriously disrupted when going into the studio. Basically, the drums are usually laid down first, then rhythm instruments, then soloists, and finally vocals. So when each musician has to conform to a click track, it can be intimidating and frustrating. This discomfort might lead you and/or the musicians you're recording to forego the click track. I would strongly dissuade you from not using the Click. Once you or the musicians get comfortable with it, it can make the difference between an average recording and a polished one.

## Configuring the Metronome

Click on the Transport menu and select Metronome Setup.

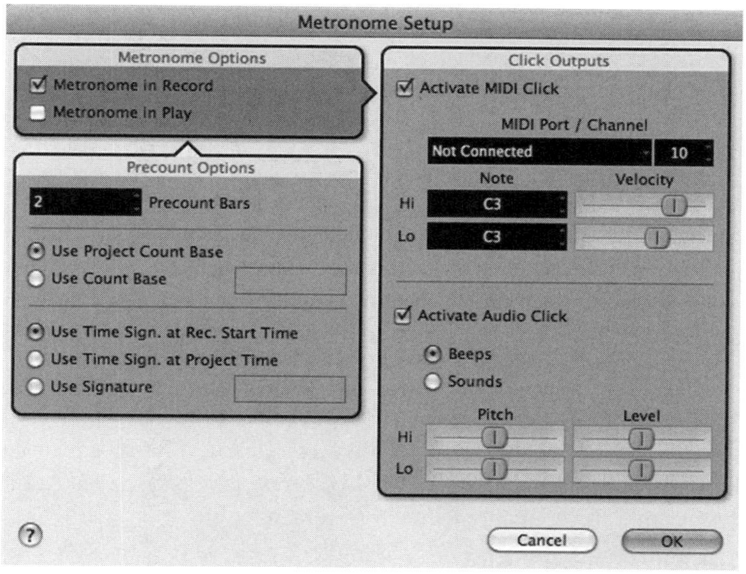

Figure 4.11: The Metronome Setup window

I would recommend the settings you see in Figure 4.11 if they're not configured this way by default. In the Metronome options, you can choose whether you hear the Click during record, playback, or both. Personally, I'd rather not hear the Click during playback unless I'm monitoring a track(s) for timing. The Precount Bars allow you to define how many bars of Click you'll hear before recording engages. Start with 2, but after you get used to the Precount, you may want to set it to 1. The MIDI Click will not be necessary, so you can disable it. However, since the default MIDI Port is Not Connected, it wouldn't be heard anyway. Make sure Activate Audio Click is enabled and set to Beeps. The Click Pitch and Level can be customized with the controls located underneath the Beeps setting. When you've made the desired settings, click the OK button to close the Metronome Setup window.

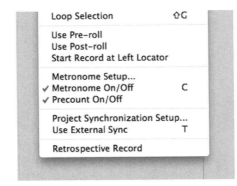

Figure 4.12: Metronome and Precount On/Off

## Metronome and Precount On/Off

You can turn the Metronome and Precount on and off by clicking on the Transport menu.

A checkmark next to each item will indicate whether the option is on or off. You'll also notice that typing "C" on your computer keyboard can toggle the Metronome On/Off. The same can be accomplished with the Click button in the Transport Panel. (See "Project Tempo and Time Signature," chapter 5.)

## Routing the Click Output

The method for defining where the Click will be sent will be handled in one of two ways. The method you choose will depend upon whether you use the Stereo Out bus in the VST Connections Outputs tab for monitoring or if you use the Control Room. (See "Assigning Audio Outputs to Cubase" and "Creating a Simple Control Room," earlier in this chapter.)

### Stereo Out Method

If you refer back to Figure 4.5, you'll notice a Click column on the right-hand side of the Outputs window. Make sure you click on the Click field directly across from the Audio Device setting. That will route the Metronome to your Stereo Out bus.

### Control Room Method (Cubase Only)

This method is only applicable if you've configured even the most modest Control Room configuration in the Studio tab of the VST Connections window. Click on the Devices menu and select Control Room Mixer.

The appearance of your Control Room Mixer may be very different than that of Figure 4.13. However, locate the Control Room Channel and make sure the CLIK button is enabled. That will allow you to hear the Click through your studio monitors as defined in the Studio tab of the VST Connections window. (See "Creating a Simple Control Room" earlier in this chapter.)

Figure 4.13: The Control Room Mixer

Note: You will also need to enable the CLIK to other Control Room Channels such as Studios and Headphones.

# Recording Some Test Tracks

Now that we have our MIDI and audio inputs and outputs configured, it's time to verify their operation by recording some test tracks. Make sure you have your "My First Project" project loaded and that it contains one MIDI track, a mono Audio track, and a stereo Audio track. If you've been following along through this chapter, you should have all three tracks created already.

## Recording a MIDI Test Track

To make this process as easy as possible, we're going to use a built-in VST Instrument as our sound-generating source. That will spare us from having to configure an external synthesizer or prematurely go over Instrument tracks. Selecting a track will usually Record Enable the track. However, if the Record Enable button is gray on the MIDI track, click on it so that it turns red.

Figure 4.14: The Record Enable button

If you were to play some notes on your MIDI controller now, you wouldn't hear anything. That's because we need to create a virtual or VST Instrument to which the MIDI track will have its output assigned. You will, however, see the MIDI Activity Indicator lighting up to show you that the track is receiving MIDI information.

### Creating a VST Instrument

Click on the Devices menu and select VST Instruments, or type F11. The VST Instruments "rack" will appear.

Figure 4.15: An empty VST Instrument rack

I call the VST Instrument window a rack because it reminds me of a nineteen-inch equipment rack into which all sorts of synthesizer modules can be mounted. We essentially do exactly that when we load a VST Instrument into one of the empty numbered slots. We just don't need cables, screws, or a physical rack to do it. To load a VST Instrument, locate the first slot, and click on the black area that contains the dim text "no instrument." A drop-down menu will appear, displaying all of the VST Instruments you can choose from.

The menu will display the virtual instruments but not the individual sounds. We'll do that in a moment. For now, click on the Synth category and then click on HALion Sonic SE. (Note: Don't be confused by the number of VST Instruments you see in the menu. I have installed a whole bunch of VST Instruments that are not part of Cubase. Your menu might not display as many choices.) You will see a dialog box asking if you'd like to create a MIDI track assigned to HALion Sonic SE. While this is great time-saving feature, hit the Cancel button for now. The HALion Sonic SE control panel will appear.

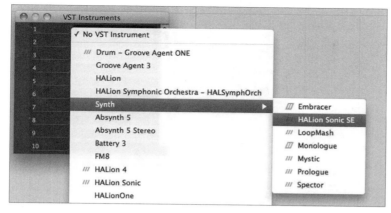

Figure 4.16: VST Instrument choices

We'll spend more time on HALion Sonic SE (hereby referred to as HSSE) later in this book. However, HSSE is a special-edition version of Steinberg's very powerful HALion Sonic Synthesizer Workstation. This SE version has a generous palette of sounds from the HALion Sonic Library. One of those sounds (First Contact) has already been loaded into Program Slot 1 by default. HSSE has 16 Program Slots, and the slot number is usually the same as the Slot MIDI Channel. However, that number can be altered at the top of the control panel. Just leave it set to "1" for now.

Figure 4.17: The upper-left quarter of the HALion Sonic SE control panel

## Setting MIDI Track Input, Output, and Channel

If you were to play some notes on your MIDI controller, you still wouldn't hear the First Contact sound. That's because we need to assign our MIDI track to HSSE on MIDI Channel 1. Go to the Inspector of MIDI track 1 and set the Track Input, Output, and Channel as they appear in Figure 4.18.

Figure 4.18: MIDI track settings for Slot 1 of HSSE & Transport controls

Once you've made those settings, you can play some notes on your MIDI controller, and you'll hear the First Contact sound. It's a synth sweep with an arpeggio layer that follows the tempo of Cubase. While it would be fun to play around with this sound, we do need to get on with the process of recording.

### Using the Transport Controls for Recording and Playback

Locate the RTZ (Return to Zero, or beginning of project) button. Go ahead and click that button to rewind the Cursor to measure 1. Click the Record button, at which point you'll hear the Metronome for the two Precount bars we previously defined in the Metronome Setup window. After the Precount, the recording will engage, and the Cursor will scroll across the display indicating the current position. A horizontal event will be drawn from left to right and will be equal to the track height. This is the event that will contain the MIDI information that you're recording and will be playing back. You won't need to worry about what you're playing on your MIDI keyboard. (We're not going to win any Grammys … yet.) Just play some notes to record the performance onto the MIDI track. When you're finished recording, click the Stop button, then the RTZ button, then click the Play button to review your recording.

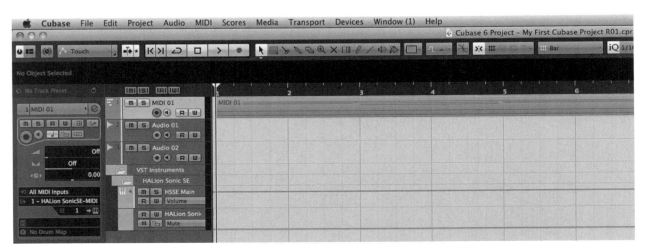

Figure 4.19: A recorded MIDI event on the MIDI track

If you didn't hear the playback, review the procedures for setting both MIDI and audio inputs and outputs. Also make sure that your audio interface is turned up and your studio monitors are powered up and have their volumes turned up too.

## Recording an Audio Test Track

Now it's time to test our audio inputs and outputs by recording an Audio track. You can use anything you want as long as it makes sound. This could be a synthesizer, vocal microphone, acoustic guitar—whatever you prefer.

### Connecting the Instrument or Microphone

A cable (or for a stereo source, you'll need two) will be required to connect the instrument or microphone to the input of your audio interface. Go ahead and make that connection. If the instrument (such as a synthesizer or acoustic guitar pickup) has a volume control, make sure it's turned all the way up. If it's a condenser microphone you'll be recording from, make sure that you enable the phantom power (+48 V) on your audio interface. (Condenser microphones require phantom power to charge the microphone capsule. Consult the owner's manuals of both the microphone and your audio interface to see if you need, and how to enable, phantom power.)

### Setting an Input Level

Your audio interface will have some sort of facility to adjust the input sensitivity or gain of its inputs. You'll usually find a knob or slider marked Gain, Level, or Volume. Setting an appropriate input level is critical for capturing the best recording possible. Fortunately, it's really easy to set. Your audio interface will probably have a peak light for every input. While you or the musician is playing or singing the loudest volume he or she will perform during the recording, turn the input gain control up until the peak light glows. Then turn the gain down until the peak light disappears. The rule is: always set the input gain as high as possible without peaking.

### Setting Audio Track Record Enable, Input, and Monitor

We made two Audio tracks in our project; one is mono and the other is stereo. Click on the Record Enable according to the number of sources required for the instrument or microphone(s) you connected to your audio interface. The example in Figure 4.20 is an acoustic guitar pickup that is a mono source; therefore, the mono track is Record Enabled.

Figure 4.20: Audio track Record Enable, Input, and Monitor settings

I double-clicked the name of the track (Audio 02) and renamed it "Qstick." (That's the silly way I label acoustic guitar tracks.) I highly recommend changing the names of your tracks, especially Audio tracks, prior to recording. Otherwise you'll end up with Audio 01 through Audio 40 and not know what any of the tracks have recorded on them.

Click on the Track Audio input and choose the desired input. For example, I plugged the acoustic guitar directly into the right input of my audio interface. Since it's mono, I set the Track Audio input to Right. (That is to say, the right bus of my Stereo In bus as defined in the Input tab of the VST Connections window.)

You might need to click the Monitor button to be able to hear the instrument or microphone prior to or during the recording. We'll go over monitoring in more detail in chapter 8. But for now, see if your audio interface has a "mix" control to balance the input and the playback. If it does, set it somewhere in the middle. (Every audio interface will provide you with the ability to monitor, but there are several methods depending on make and model. You may also need to consult the owner's manual of your audio interface to learn how it facilitates monitoring.)

### Recording the Audio Track

Review Figure 4.18 for the location of the Transport controls. Then you can refer to "Using the Transport Controls for Recording and Playback" (earlier in this chapter) to learn how to record and review your track; only this time you'll be recording audio, and an Audio event will appear in the Event window.

Figure 4.21: A recorded Audio event on the Audio track

Press the Play button to review your recording. (If you can't hear the Audio track, try disabling the Monitor button.) Now you'll hear the MIDI track (if you recorded one) and the Audio track simultaneously. If your Audio event doesn't display a waveform of the recording or you can't hear the playback, review this chapter and verify your settings.

# Anticipating the Possibilities

If everything was configured properly, you just made your first recording with Cubase! You should be feeling empowered and ready to forge on. I hope you are, because you can create a lot of music with the simple operations you've learned so far. However, there's a lot more to Cubase, and I hope you're ready to learn more.

## DVD Option #1

If you'd like to hear what I came up with for "My First Cubase Project" project, you will find that project inside of its Project Folder on the DVD that came with this book. You might be interested to hear how your inspiration differed from mine. I added another Audio track, upon which I recorded a bass guitar. (Be kind in your critique of my project, for I have been writing this book and not practicing my guitar or bass skills.)

# Chapter 5

# THE PROJECT WINDOW AND TRANSPORT PANEL

The Project Window is where you'll be spending most of your time while working in Cubase. Think of it as the driver's seat of a new automobile, for that is the place in which you spend the most time in your car. Since this car is new, you'll have to learn how to start the engine, where the operational controls are, how to tune to your favorite radio station, and how to set the climate controls. (You'll notice how I put music before comfort; I do have my priorities straight, you know.) Cubase is the same way, except you've already learned how to "start the car" by launching Cubase. Now you'll need to learn where all the operational controls and features are. In this chapter, you will learn about:

- The three columns of the Project window.
- The Time Ruler.
- The Left and Right Locators.
- How to set the Window Layout options.
- The Inspector and Toolbar, Status, Info, and Overview Lines.
- The Transport Panel and the numeric keypad.

## The Project Window

Before we can talk about the Project window, we'll need to start a new project. Up to this point, we've been using "My First Cubase Project." If you still have it loaded, close that project so that we can focus on a new, empty project. You'll also need to know how to add tracks to a project, so make sure to review those steps in chapter 4. Basically, you can create tracks by clicking the Project menu and selecting Add Track, or by right-clicking in the Track column. (See Figure 5.1.)

Click on the File menu, and select New Project. Then follow the procedures described in "The Project Assistant," chapter 3, to create a new project named "Project and Transport." You should now see an empty Project window, as shown in Figure 5.1.

Figure 5.1: An empty project

The Project window is comprised of several columns and rows similar to a spreadsheet. (The rows are referred to as *lines*, which we will discuss shortly.) Make sure that you can see all three columns, including the Inspector. If you can only see two columns, click the Window Layout button (second button from the left on the toolbar) and make sure that Inspector has a checkmark next to it. (To close the Window Layout, click anywhere outside of the window or wait about seven seconds.) Let's talk about the three main columns of the Project window.

## Inspector

The first column is called the Inspector. The Inspector contains all of the settings for each individual track. Those settings are located within sections that appear within the Inspector. The sections found within the Inspector will vary depending on the type of track you have selected. In other words, an Audio track will have an Inserts section, while a MIDI track will have a MIDI Inserts section. The former will have an Equalizers section, while the latter will not. Other specialized tracks (such as Markers and Tempo) will have unique sections that won't appear for any other track. For now, let's talk about the sections for MIDI and Audio tracks. Go ahead and click on the Project menu, select Add Track, and then click on MIDI Track. The Add MIDI Track dialog box will appear, wherein you will set the Count to 1, then click the Add Track button. Repeat the process, but this time add one mono or stereo Audio track.

### MIDI Track Inspector Sections

Make sure that you have the MIDI track selected to reveal the MIDI sections as shown in Figure 5.2.

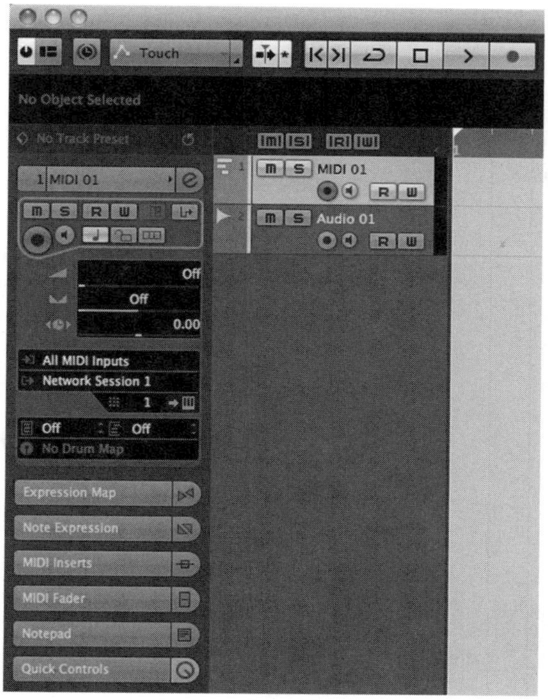

Figure 5.2: The MIDI track sections

The top section will be easy to spot, because it has the same name and color as the MIDI track. In this example, it's MIDI 01. If you cannot see the settings within the top section, click on the section to reveal the settings that appear in Figure 5.2. The top section contains the most common settings for a MIDI track, including Track Controls, Volume, Pan, Input & Output (see "Cubasic #2: Assigning MIDI Inputs and Outputs to Tracks," chapter 4), and so on. Underneath those settings, you will see the remaining sections: Expression Map, Note Expression, MIDI Inserts, MIDI Fader, Notepad, and Quick Controls. Click on any section to reveal the settings. When you do, the top section will become hidden, and the selection section will be revealed. (You can also Ctrl/Command + click to reveal or hide multiple section settings, or Alt/Option + click to reveal or hide all of the sections.) For now, click on the top section so that the Inspector appears as it does in Figure 5.2.

## Audio Track Inspector Sections

Now make sure you have the Audio track selected to reveal the Audio sections as shown in Figure 5.3.

The settings that appear in the top section of an Audio track are very similar to those of a MIDI track, especially the Track controls such as Record Enable, Monitor, Input, and Output. However, there are some new sections we haven't seen before, including Inserts, Equalizers, Sends, and Channel. Click on any section to reveal the corresponding settings. The Notepad and Quick Control sections are common to both MIDI and Audio tracks. The behaviors of revealing and hiding Audio track sections are identical to those of MIDI tracks.

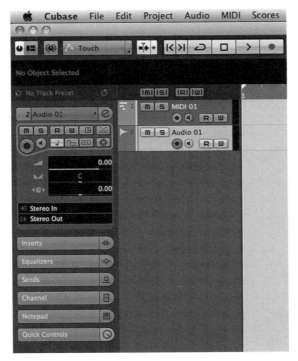

Figure 5.3: The Audio track sections

## Instrument Track Inspector Sections

We haven't worked with an Instrument track yet. However, due to the popularity of virtual instruments, I think you'll use it more often than its cousin, the MIDI track. An Instrument track starts with MIDI data and ends with audio data. It's basically a MIDI track and an Audio track with a virtual synthesizer in between. A virtual instrument sandwich, if you will. (Great, now I'm hungry.) Therefore, you'll find many of the same sections used by both MIDI and Audio tracks. Go ahead and click on the Project menu, select Add Track, and then select Instrument. The Add Instrument Track dialog box will appear. Locate and click on the Add Track button without making any other selections within the dialog box; save the Count of 1. You will now see a third track added to your Track column as it appears in Figure 5.4.

You will find MIDI sections such as Expression Map and Note Expression along with Audio sections such as Inserts and Equalizers. The top section is identical to a MIDI track. The behaviors of revealing and hiding Instrument track sections are identical to those of MIDI and Audio tracks.

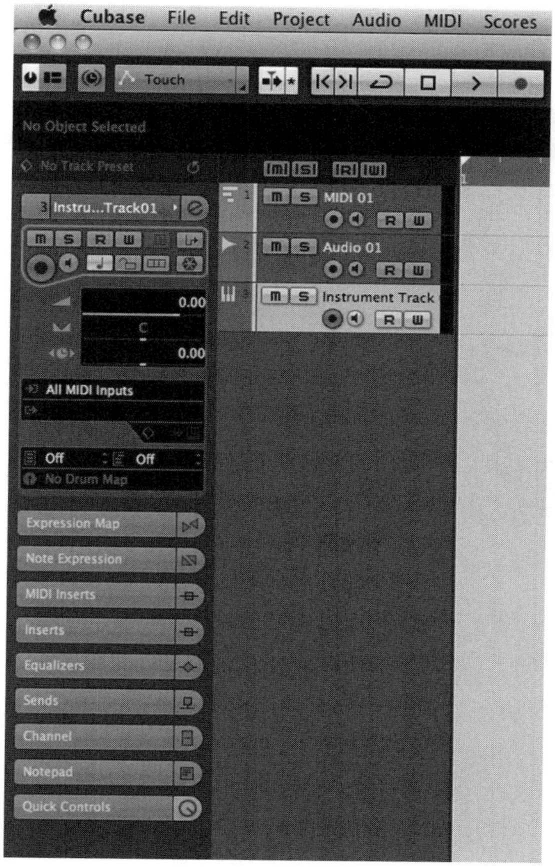

Figure 5.4: The Instrument track sections

## Track Column

To the right of the Inspector you will find the Track Column. (See Figure 5.1) We've already added three tracks to this Project: one MIDI, one Audio, and one Instrument. Clicking on a track will reveal its sections and settings in the Inspector.

### Changing the Track Name

The track itself has a name that you can change by double-clicking on the default name and typing the desired name, followed by typing the Enter key on your computer keyboard. I strongly recommend naming each track immediately after its creation. If you don't, you'll end up with a bunch of tracks with default names, such as MIDI 01 through MIDI 40. If you don't name the track, you'll have to listen to each one to determine what it contains, and that will certainly slow your workflow. Simple names are the best, such as "Lead Vocal 1" or "Drum OH Left." However, if your names get longer than about fourteen characters, the Track name field will be contracted. But you can hover your mouse over the Track name to have the entire name crawl (like the text at the bottom of a cable news broadcast) from right to left.

### Altering Track Height

When you hover your mouse over a track (upper or lower) boundary, the pointer will turn into an icon resembling two horizontal parallel lines with one arrow pointing up and one pointing down. Now click and drag the lower boundary of a track to increase the track height, as in the Instrument track in Figure 5.5.

Figure 5.5: Altering the track height

You can also hold Ctrl/Command to adjust the height of all tracks simultaneously. Or holding Shift + Alt/Option will adjust the height of all tracks below the track you've selected to adjust.

There are also controls for adjusting the height of all tracks simultaneously. In the lower right-hand corner of the Project window, you will find the Zoom controls, as seen in Figure 5.6.

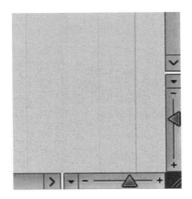

Figure 5.6: Track Zoom controls

Moving the vertical Zoom slider up or down will adjust the height of all tracks. Clicking on the Zoom In or Zoom Out will alter track height in steps. There is also the Track Zoom presets button. Clicking on that button will reveal the Track Zoom presets menu, as seen in Figure 5.7.

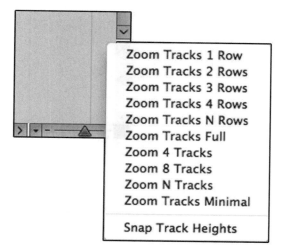

Figure 5.7: Track Zoom presets menu open

The Track presets allow you to quickly conform all the tracks to predefined heights. For example, clicking on Zoom 8 Tracks will quickly adjust the height so that eight tracks will be visible in the Project window.

When you increase the track height, you'll be able to see more Track Controls. The Track Controls will vary by the track type. Increase the height of all three tracks so that they appear like Figure 5.8.

Figure 5.8: The most commonly used Track Controls

### Track Controls for Individual Tracks

Track Controls are the little buttons that appear on the track itself. There are many different Track Controls, and they'll vary depending on track type. However, there are several commonly used Track Controls I'd like to describe. (Note: Multiple Track Controls can be used simultaneously across multiple tracks.)

Mute disables the playback so that you don't hear the material recorded on the track.

Solo allows you to hear only the track that is soloed.

Record Enable will allow new material to be recorded the next time you hit the Record button on the Transport Panel. (See "The Transport Panel," later in this chapter.)

Monitor allows you to hear the track as it's being recorded. Monitor is used mostly on Audio tracks, and its behavior depends greatly on your Monitor strategy. (See "Choosing a Monitoring Strategy," chapter 8.)

Edit Channel Settings will open the Track Channel Setting control panel.

Read Enable will set the track to play back automation data.

Write Enable will set the track to record automation data.

Track Type Icon is not a Track Control but does indicate the track type. The icons are identical to the icons in the Add Track command.

### Track Controls for All Tracks

At the top of the Track Column, you will find four Track Controls that affect all tracks simultaneously. These are great when you want to disable all active Mutes or Solos, or disable all reading and/or writing of automation data.

## Event Display Column

The Event Display contains visual representations of all the data you record or enter into your Cubase Project. The events may be MIDI or audio data, but can also be automation or MIDI controls data. When we start recording, the types of data and their representation in the Event Display will become more obvious.

### The Ruler

The Ruler represents the timeline of your project and is shown in Figure 5.9.

The Ruler depicts the temporal measurement of the data in the Event Display, with earlier events to the left and later events to the right. The default time unit is Bars + Beats and is the most musical of representations. You can click on the Ruler Options button (far right of the ruler) and select a different unit of measurement, such as Timecode or Seconds.

Figure 5.9: The Ruler, Ruler options, and Waveform Zoom slider

### Waveform Zoom

When editing audio data, it can be difficult to see the quiet passages. The Waveform Zoom slider allows you to adjust the height, not of the Audio track, but of the waveform display of the events. It has no effect on nonaudio data. The default slider position is at its lowest position. Moving the slider up will increase the waveform height. While it will make your waveforms look louder, no volume or gain adjustments are occurring.

## Event Zoom Controls

Similarly to the Event zoom options, there are multiple ways of zooming the Event Display. My favorite way is a little difficult to describe. But once you've used it, you'll wish every software program zoomed the same way. Click on the Ruler, and hold your mouse button. Then push your mouse upward to zoom out, or pull it down to zoom in. Once the preferred zoom level has been achieved, release your mouse button.

You can also increment or decrement the zoom by typing "G" to zoom out or "H" to zoom in. Plus, there are Zoom controls located in the lower right-hand corner of the Project window, as shown in Figure 5.10.

Figure 5.10: The Event zoom controls

Most Event zoom controls work similarly to their Track zoom counterparts but alter the scale of the timeline rather than the track height. However, the zoom presets are a bit different, as you'll see in Figure 5.11.

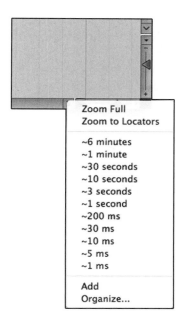

Figure 5.11: The Event zoom presets

The Event zoom presets are always depicted in minutes, seconds, or ms (milliseconds), regardless of the Ruler units setting. I like to think of them as "show me X amount of time in the Event Display." For example, choosing ~1 minute will zoom the display to a one-minute region. A setting of ~30 seconds will zoom the display to a thirty-second region, and so on. (Note: You can also perform an Event zoom in the Overview Line, which will be discussed later in this chapter.

### The Cursor

The Cursor indicates the current temporal position within the project. For example, click on measure 2 within the Ruler of your Cubase Project. The Cursor will move to the position of measure 2, as in Figure 5.12.

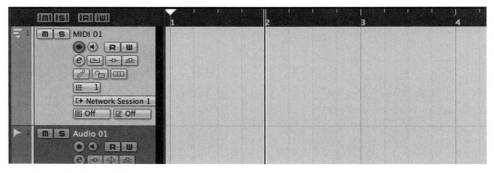

Figure 5.12: The Cursor with Snap on

Moving the Cursor allows you to select a temporal location where you can start recording or playback. It's similar to fast-forwarding or rewinding, except that it instantly locates the Cursor to the position you choose on the Ruler. The precision with which the Cursor (and as you'll learn later, Locators and Events) is placed on the Ruler is determined by the Snap.

### Cubasic #5: Snap

Snap will allow for precision placement of the Cursor, Locators, and Events. (The latter two you will learn about a little later.) Snap is normally enabled by default, which means that when you placed the Cursor at measure 2, it magnetically snapped the measure. There may be times when more or less precision is required. Such situations would require a modification of the Snap settings or disabling Snap altogether. Those settings are located at the top of the Cubase Project window, as shown in Figure 5.13.

Figure 5.13: The Snap settings

You can turn the Snap on and off completely by clicking the Snap On/Off button or by typing "J" on your computer keyboard. To alter the precision of the Snap when it's on, click on the Grid Type button. The default setting is Bar, which means that Snap will place the Cursor or other items to the nearest bar. But a Grid Type of Beat will allow the Snap to place items on the nearest quarter-note beat within a bar. Or for further precision, the setting of Use Quantize will conform the Snap to the currently selected Quantize Preset. The default of 1/16 will set the precision to sixteenth-notes. (Note: The Grid Type and Quantize Preset setting will have no effect when the Snap is off.)

### Cubasic #6: Auto-Scroll

Auto-Scroll constantly updates the event display and the Cursor position during recording, playback, and editing. I find myself leaving Auto-Scroll on practically all the time, because I like to see the events during recording and playback. During editing, however, Auto-Scroll can unexpectedly move the display, leaving you wondering where your data went. Steinberg added a new behavior to the Auto-Scroll that makes it possible to edit events while leaving Auto-Scroll on. The Auto-Scroll button can be located in the upper left-hand corner of the Project window, as seen in Figure 5.14.

Figure 5.14: Auto-Scroll buttons

Both Auto-Scroll and Suspend Auto-Scroll when Editing buttons are enabled by default. You can disable Auto-Scroll either by clicking the button or by typing "F" on your computer keyboard. I would recommend leaving Suspend Auto-Scroll when Editing enabled at all times. If you turn it off, Auto-Scroll can unceremoniously reposition the Event Display and Cursor while you're trying to edit something and can cause a lot of consternation. Prior to Cubase 5, there was no Suspend feature, which required you to either stop playback or turn off Auto-Scroll (formerly Follow, hence the key command of "F") if you wanted to edit and continue playback at the same time.

## Cubasic #7: The Left and Right Locators

At first, the Locators can be a little challenging to understand and work with. But they are equally useful and necessary; therefore, learning to use them will be critical for a variety of operations. When you start recording in a new Cubase Project, chances are you won't be continuously recording from the very beginning of a track to the very end. Throughout history, composers have compartmentalized their work so that they could focus on each section, each instrument, and every note. Focusing is exactly what the Locators do: restrict the attention of both the user and the program to a specific region of the Event Display.

The Left and Right Locators are found on the Ruler; however, by default they might both be located at bar 1. That makes them a little hard to see, as shown in Figure 5.15.

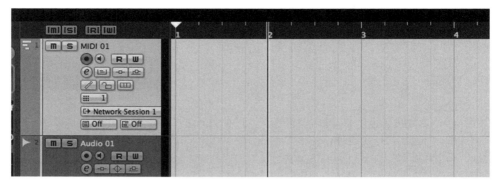

Figure 5.15: Locators both at bar 1

The Locators appear as small triangle shapes in the Ruler. When they're back to back as they are in Figure 5.14, they make one bigger triangle and are impossible to differentiate from one another. They won't be of much use to you until you move them.

## Positioning the Locators

Before we start moving the Locators, make sure that your Snap is on and that the Grid Type is set to Bar. Next, there are a multitude of methods for moving the Locators. I find myself using all of the methods during the course of a project, except one:

### Dragging

While it is possible and seemingly logical to click and drag each Locator to the desired position, I would dissuade you from using this method. Personally, I find it to be cumbersome. However, if dragging the Locators works for you, don't let me stop you.

### Clicking

This is by far my favorite method. It involves clicking on the Ruler while holding a modifier key on your computer keyboard. To position the Left Locator, type and hold Ctrl/Option, and then click on the Ruler. To position the Right Locator, type and hold Alt/Command, and then click on the Ruler.

### Using the Keypad

By keypad, I'm talking about the numeric keypad that is located on the right-hand side of a full-sized computer keyboard. Having a keypad is critical for transport control of Cubase. (We'll learn more about the Transport Panel and the keypad in the next section.) If you are using a laptop or have an abbreviated keyboard without a keypad (such as the Apple Wireless Keyboard), I would strongly recommend that you get a USB or Bluetooth (if your computer has Bluetooth capabilities) keypad.

Start by moving the Cursor to the desired position by clicking on the Ruler. Then type Ctrl/Command + 1 (the "1" on the keypad) to place the Left Locator at the Cursor position. Repeat the process for the Right Locator, but this time type Ctrl/Command + 2. (The use of the keypad "1" and "2" keys will become apparent in the next section.) I find the keypad method a little slower than the clicking method. But it's very useful if your cursor happens to be positioned where you'd like to place a Locator.

### Proper Locator Positioning

It's important to note that the Left Locator must always be placed to the left of the Right Locator, and the Right Locator always placed to the right of the Left Locator. If I've succeeded in confusing you with this directional dichotomy, let me illustrate what

I'm talking about with Figures 5.16 and 5.17. In both cases, the Locators are placed at bars 2 and 4.

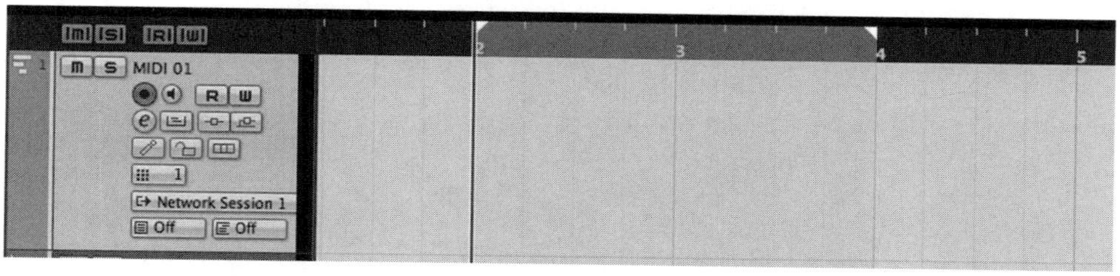

Figure 5.16: Proper Locator positioning

It's easy to see when the Locators are placed properly, because there will be a blue region displayed in the Ruler between the Locators.

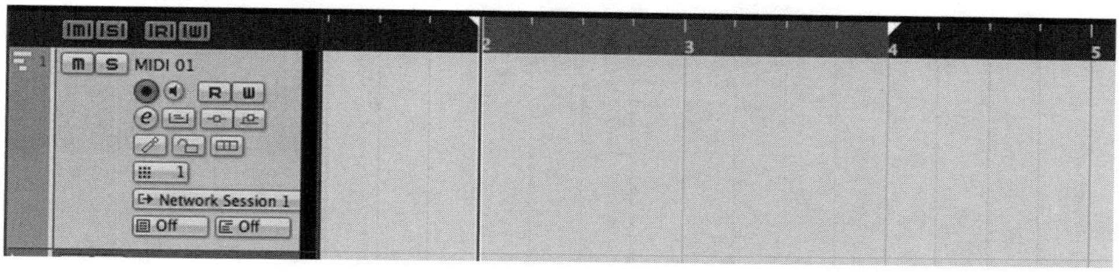

Figure 5.17: Reversed Locator positioning

When the Locator positions are reversed, two things will happen. First, the region on the Ruler will be red, indicating reversed Locator positioning. Second, certain operations (such as Audio Export and Mixdown) will be impossible. Therefore, it's very important to keep the Left Locator on the left and the Right Locator on the right.

# Toolbar, Status, Info, and Overview Lines

Now that we've gone over the three columns of the Project window, we need to discuss the rows that make up the Toolbar, Status, Info, and Overview Lines. You can think of them as the vertical rows of a spreadsheet. They're all made visible or hidden with the Window Layout settings. See Figure 5.18 for the location of the Window Layout button, and click on it.

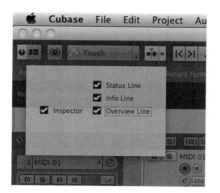

Figure 5.18: The Window Layout settings

When you reveal the Window Layout settings, the Project window will become covered in opaque blue. This is a behavior you will see during some Cubase operations, and is normal. It basically means there's a screen visible that may need your attention before proceeding. In the case of the Window Layout, make sure that the Inspector is still checked, along with the Status, Info, and Overview Lines. You'll see a few vertical rows appear across the top of the Project window. Then you can click in the opaque blue area to return to the Project window, or you can wait about seven seconds, and the Window Layout will close itself.

Figure 5.19: The Toolbar, Status, Info, and Overview Lines

Since we don't have anything in our Project and Transport Project yet, I'm going to load a project that has some material already recorded in it. That project, along with all the lines, is depicted in Figure 5.19.

Each of these lines depicts different data, and all but the Toolbar can be configured on a project-by-project basis.

## Toolbar

The Toolbar is visible at all times. It's the Cubase equivalent of a handyman's tool belt. Basically, it's where you keep the tools. Take a look at some of the buttons on the Toolbar. We've already used ones such as the basic transport controls, Auto-Scroll, and Snap settings.

## Status Line

The Status Line contains the basic Project settings such as Record Format and Project Frame Rate. It also contains the Record Time Max indicator that displays how much recording time you have left on your hard disk. In Figure 5.19, it reads 852 hours and 52 minutes. (I guess I need to get recording!) Clicking on the reading will open a separate Record Time Max display that can be repositioned on your computer monitor (or second monitor) anywhere you'd like.

## Project Setup

The other settings displayed in the Status Line are part of the Project Setup. Clicking on anything other than the Record Time Max indicator will open the Project Setup window, as show in Figure 5.20. The Project Setup window can also be accessed from the Project menu or by typing Shift + S.

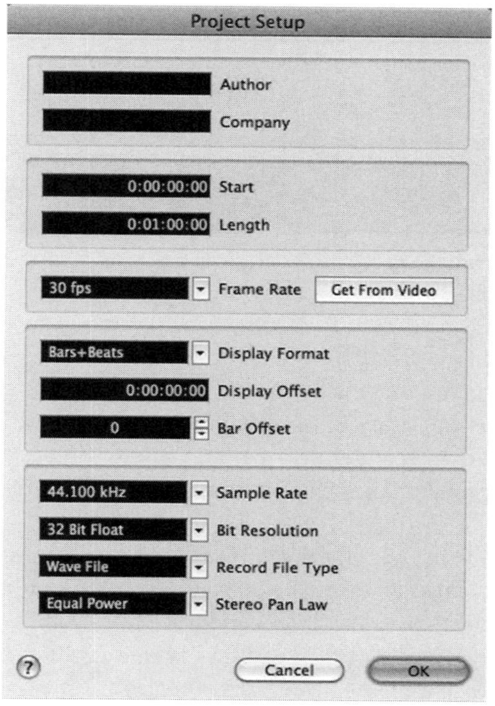

Figure 5.20: The Project Setup window

Pay particular attention to the four settings in the bottom of the Project Setup window. They are the settings displayed in the Status Line. Unless you have the specific need to use different values, I would recommend using the settings as they appear in Figure 5.20.

## Info Line

When you click on an event in the Event Display, the Info Line will display very detailed information about the event. For example, the event selected in Figure 5.19 is an Audio event. In the Info Line, you can see the File Name and Description, along with very detailed timing information, such as Start, End, Length, and Offset. Clicking on any field will allow you to edit the text and/or timing values.

## Overview Line

The Overview Line has two basic functions. First, it provides a very small-scale display of the Event Display and can give you an idea of where you are in the project. Second, you can click and drag across the Overview Line to perform an Event zoom.

# The Transport Panel

In the previous chapter, we used the Transport controls in the Toolbar for Play, Stop, and Return to Zero. But there are a great many more Transport controls, all of which appear in the Transport Panel. The Transport Panel is an independent floating window that is visible by default. If you cannot see it in your Project window, click the Transport menu and select Transport Panel, or type F2 on your computer keyboard. The appearance of the Transport Panel may vary from that of Figure 5.21, but the controls we will be discussing are visible by default.

Figure 5.21: The Transport Panel

## Primary and Secondary Time Displays

By default, the Primary and Secondary Time Displays are set to Bars + Beats, and Seconds, respectively. They provide a constant readout of the Cursor position at all times. You can click on a digit in either readout to enter a value to locate to. You can also hover your pointer slightly above any value and click to increment, or slightly below any value and click to decrement.

To the right of the digital readouts is an icon showing the current format. Clicking that icon will allow you to change the format. For example, if you're working on a project that is based on timecode, you could click on the Secondary Time Display format icon and choose Timecode. At the division of the readouts is the Exchange Time Formats button that will exchange the placement of the Time Displays.

## Main Transport Controls

The main Transport controls are pretty self-explanatory. However, there may be some functions with which you're not familiar. Let's cover all those bases by referring to Figure 5.22, and go from left to right.

Figure 5.22: The main Transport controls

### Go to Previous Marker/Zero

Since we haven't inserted any Markers into our Project and Transport Project, this button will return the Cursor to the very beginning of the project. This is also known as RTZ, or Return to Zero, but Cubase refers to it as Zero. If your project does have Markers, clicking this button will move the Cursor backward, stopping at every Marker.

### Go to Next Marker/Project End

This button works the same as the Go to Previous Marker/Zero button, except that it moves the Cursor forward in time. Clicking the button will move the Cursor to the end of the project or forward, stopping at every Marker, if present.

### Rewind

You can click or click and hold on the Rewind button to move the Cursor backward in time. The speed of the rewind is determined by the current Event zoom setting. In other words, the more zoomed out the Event Display, the faster the rewind will proceed.

### Forward

The Forward button functions identically to the Rewind button but moves the Cursor forward in time.

### Cycle

Cycle is a Cubase mode wherein the Cursor plays (or records) repeatedly through a predetermined time range. That range is determined by the placement of the Left and Right Locators; the Left Locator is the start of the Cycle, and the Right Locator is the end of the Cycle. The Cycle button enables or disables the Cycle mode. When enabled, the button will be purple, but it will be gray when disabled.

### Stop

The Stop button has two behaviors, depending on whether playback is engaged or not. During playback, clicking Stop will discontinue playback, and the Cursor will remain at the current location. However, if playback is already disengaged, clicking the Stop button will locate the Cursor to the previous playback location. For example, if you start playback at measure 10 and press stop when the Cursor reaches measure 15, the Cursor will remain at measure 15. Pressing stop again will move the Cursor back to measure 10. This is very useful for playing back or recording a section several times without using Cycle mode with the Left and Right Locators. (If I were recording, I would definitely employ the Locators.) The default color of the Stop button is amber.

### Play (Start)

Weirdly, the Play button is sometimes referred to in Cubase as "Start." Either way, pressing the Play button will start playback. During playback, the Play button will be green, but if playback is stopped, it will be gray.

### Record

Clicking the Record button will start the recording process for any and all tracks that are record enabled. Recording can occur either from a stopped position or during playback. The former will result in the Precount (if enabled) occurring before recording proceeds. The Record button itself is gray with a red dot in the center but will be completely red during recording.

# Cubasic #8: Transport and the Keypad

As I previously mentioned, having a keypad when you're using Cubase is critical. That's because the Transport controls are tied to the keypad as key commands. Have a look at Figure 5.23 to see what I mean.

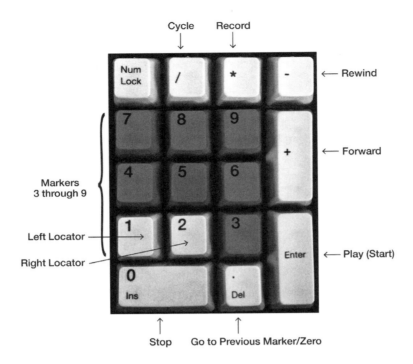

Figure 5.23: The keypad and associated Transport controls

The Transport controls are usually the most frequently used Cubase buttons. Basically, you'll be hitting buttons such as Play, Stop, and Record a lot. And if you rely on the Transport Panel for all of these commands, you'll need to grab your mouse and move the pointer to each button every time. That makes using Cubase much more laborious than it needs to be. You will find using the keypad a much faster way of accessing your Transport controls. The concept is what I call the "mouseless recording workflow," and we'll be using that workflow when we start recording in chapter 7. On the disc that accompanies this book, you will find a PDF folder that contains a file named "Keypad and Transport.pdf." It is a printable version of Figure 5.23 and shows the keypad and its associated Transport controls. Please print that PDF, and place it where you can easily see it.

## The Spacebar

The Spacebar is the largest key on your computer keyboard. It is a Transport control, even though it's not located on the keypad. It operates as a Play/Stop toggle. In other words, if Cubase is stopped, typing the Spacebar will start playback. Type Spacebar during playback, and Cubase will stop.

## The Left and Right Locators on the Keypad

The Locators are not found in the Main Transport controls of the Transport Panel. They appear to the left of the Main Transport and are labeled "L" and "R." But as with the Transport controls, moving the cursor to the Left or Right Locator positions is much faster with the keypad. Simply type "1" or "2" to move the Cursor to the Left and Right Locators respectively.

## Yes, We Have No Keypads

I also previously mentioned that many laptops and some keyboards (such as the Apple Wireless Keyboard) don't have keypads. On laptops, the keypad is sometimes located on the keyboard and can be accessed by holding the "fn" (function) key on the keyboard and then typing the key. The keypad keys are usually listed on the keyboard in the same color as the fn key. For example, if the fn letters are blue, look for similarly colored numbers on the keyboard.

While the fn method works, it's not … well … fun. It requires that you use both hands to type one keypad key. To that end, let's explore some other options.

### Adding a Keyboard or Keypad

The answer might be as simple as adding a full-sized keyboard that has a keypad. USB keyboards are very inexpensive. Or if you're space limited, you could look for a USB or Bluetooth keypad. (Your computer would need to be Bluetooth-equipped for the latter to be a viable option.) However, make sure that you can return the keypad to the store, just in case it's incompatible. You see, I've seen some keypads that don't type the right keys. In other words, typing the keypad "1" instead types the "1" on the top row of keyboard keys. When that happens, you're not moving the Left Locator, you're accessing the Toolbar pointer. Test the keypad thoroughly with Cubase before tossing your receipt in the recycle basket.

### The Steinberg CC121

Steinberg makes a USB controller for Cubase (and Nuendo) called the CC121.

Figure 5.24: The Steinberg CC121 Cubase/Nuendo controller

It not only provides the Transport controls, but also adds lightning-fast control of other Cubase parameters such as Fader, Pan, Track Controls, EQ, shuttle/jog, and Control Room volume. Plus, you can hover your pointer over any control on Cubase and adjust it by turning the CC121 AI (Advanced Integration) knob. The CC121 is made of metal and a real joy to use. However, if it's out of your price range, Steinberg created the Cubase iC app.

### The Cubase iC App for iPhone, iPod Touch, and iPad

Who can argue with free? (Well, I've met many who can, but I digress…) For the Apple products listed above, Steinberg made the free Cubase iC app, which is available from the Apple App Store.

Figure 5.25: The Cubase iC control panel

Cubase iC requires your Apple device and computer to be connected to a router with Wi-Fi. Your computer doesn't have to connect via a Wi-Fi connection, but it must be connected to the router to which the device running Cubase iC is connected.

### Saitara Software for iPhone, iPod Touch, and iPad

While their apps aren't free, Saitara Software makes some really killer apps that control Cubase Transport, Faders, Pan, EQ, and a myriad of others. Most of their apps are under $10, so they're very affordable. The connection requirements are identical to those of Cubase iC. However, they work faster when your computer creates its own Wi-Fi network to which the Apple device connects. You can get more information and check out their AC-7 family of apps at http://www.saitarasoftware.com.

# Project Tempo and Time Signature

Cubase has two different modes that control the tempo of a project: fixed tempo or variable via the Tempo track. Either method can be adjusted at any time. However, you should be aware that altering the tempo of a project that contains Audio tracks will have some seemingly strange results. You see, altering the Project tempo will have no effect on the tempo of Audio tracks. MIDI and Instrument tracks will follow tempo changes, but Audio tracks will play back at the tempo at which they were recorded. There are methods for adjusting the tempo of audio data, but it usually results in audible artifacts. Therefore, make sure you're happy with your tempo settings prior to recording your first Audio track.

Located to the right of the Transport buttons on the Transport Panel are the tempo and time signature settings, as seen in Figure 5.26.

Figure 5.26: Tempo and time signature settings

### Tempo Fixed

By default, Cubase has its Tempo mode set to Track with an establishing tempo of 120 BPM (beats per minute). However, many pop songs maintain the same tempo throughout the entire composition. That tempo probably won't be 120 BPM. For this reason, you can click on the Tempo button to switch from Track mode to Fixed. Then you can double-click on the Tempo value and enter the desired BPM amount. For now, since we're still working on some of the basics, set the mode to Fixed. That way you can quickly change the Tempo while you're working with MIDI or Instrument tracks.

### Tempo Track

We've already discussed the three most common tracks: MIDI, Instrument, and Audio. But there's also a track known as the Tempo track. This track exists in every Cubase Project even if you haven't added it manually. The Tempo track can be displayed within the Track column, or by clicking on the Project menu and selecting Tempo track, or by typing Ctrl/Command + T.

### Time Signature

The Tempo track also contains time signature changes. Since the Tempo track is on by default, it contains an establishing time signature of 4/4. But since we'll be using the Tempo Fixed mode, the default value of 4/4 will appear in the time signature setting in the Transport Panel. If you prefer to change the value, double-click on the current time signature setting and enter the desired value. Make sure to separate the integers with the "/" (forward slash) key.

# VST Performance Meters

Cubase offers two meters that constantly monitor the performance of your computer. These meters can be used to identify performance issues that can appear as audible anomalies such as pops, clicks, static, and dropouts. There is an ASIO meter and a DISK meter, and these are located at the far left of the Transport Panel, as in Figure 5.27.

Figure 5.27: The ASIO and DISK meters in the Transport Panel

Each is a ladder-style meter, but they display different performance aspects.

### ASIO Meter

The ASIO (Audio Streaming Input/Output) meter displays how much computer processing power Cubase is using to create your project. The need for power increases when you add more Audio tracks, VST Instruments, EQ, effects, and other plug-ins to a project. It will also increase if you import a video file onto a Video track. As you add more power-hungry components to a project, the ASIO meter will climb higher. Think of it like the tachometer on your car: the higher the meter, the more power you're using ... and there's a limit.

The limit is reached when the red overload indicator appears at the top of the meter. When it appears, you'll start to hear the pops, clicks, and other anomalies. Just like with a car—if you red-line the tachometer, you won't be moving any faster (at least, not in the current gear). But with the ASIO meter, the overload indicator tells you when the amount of processing power you're demanding has exceeded the design specification of your computer. There are ways to lower the demand, such as lowering the ASIO buffer size. (See "Setting The Lowest Possible Buffer Size" and "Keeping Your Latency Expectations Realistic" in chapter 8). However, if you've taken all the possible steps to conserve processing power, the ultimate solution would be to purchase a computer with a faster CPU or multiple processor cores.

### DISK Meter

The DISK meter is similar to the ASIO meter, except that instead of monitoring processing power, it measures disk throughput. Think of it as a highway with multiple lanes: the more lanes, the more cars or "traffic" can move along the highway without causing a traffic jam. (You Californians know what I'm talking about.) The faster your hard drive, the more throughput it is capable of. It allows you to record and play back more and more Audio tracks. (Note: Today's hard drives are so fast that you may only see the DISK meter when working on projects with high Audio track counts.) And as with the ASIO meter, audible anomalies will appear when the DISK overload light comes on (or to perpetuate the metaphor, people start honking in a traffic jam).

There are ways to increase disk throughput, such as defragmenting the drive. However, if you're encountering the overload indicator frequently, it might be time for a faster hard drive. I recommend the Western Digital Caviar Black series of hard drives.

### VST Performance Window

The ASIO and DISK meters on the Transport Panel are quite small. Therefore, Cubase has another way to view the meters in the VST Performance window that can be accessed by clicking on the Devices menu and selecting VST Performance or typing F12.

This is a floating window that can be placed anywhere on your computer monitor(s). The meters are identical to those found in the Transport Panel, except that they're oriented horizontally and are much bigger for easier and more accurate analysis.

## Moving On to MIDI

While MIDI itself hasn't changed much in the decades since its invention, the way we use it in Cubase has changed dramatically. With that in mind, let's learn about the concepts of MIDI and VST (virtual) Instruments in the next chapter.

Figure 5.28: The VST Performance window

# Chapter **6**

# A PRIMER ON MIDI AND VIRTUAL INSTRUMENTS

**M**IDI (Musical Instrument Digital Interface) has been around since 1983. It is a computer-based protocol and language that interconnects all sorts of electronic musical instruments, including computers and music software. It helped revolutionize the home and project recording studio. Musicians and composers could finally record, edit, process, and mix music without the need to book time in a recording studio. You can do the same thing with Cubase; plus the powerful virtual instruments give Cubase a built-in palette of sounds to choose from. In this chapter, you will learn about:

- The basics of MIDI.
- The most commonly used MIDI data.
- How sound is generated by hardware and virtual instruments.
- The concepts of monotimbral and multitimbral synthesizers.

## The Basics of MIDI

The MIDI Specification has been modified and refined over the years. But for the most part, the basic concepts remain unaltered. So even though MIDI has been around for almost thirty years, it is by no means an obsolete format. However, the concepts of MIDI are still a little difficult for beginners. To that end, I want to describe to you what MIDI is. The easiest way to start is to tell you what MIDI isn't.

### MIDI Is Not Sound

The biggest misconception about MIDI is that it is sound. While it is true that you can record MIDI data onto MIDI and Instrument tracks, the sound itself is not captured. What is captured are the actions of the performer. What do I mean by "actions"? Well, let me illustrate by having you look at your computer keyboard. When you're writing an email, the program is capturing the keystrokes from your keyboard. In other words, when you type the letter "B," the computer records that key being pressed. It does not record the sound the letter makes, nor would it record a word beginning with that letter, such as *beekeeper*. The only data captured by the computer is that of the "B" key as you type it.

Now take a look at your MIDI Keyboard. When you're recording a MIDI track in Cubase and you press a "B" key on your MIDI Keyboard, the sound itself is not captured. Instead, Cubase records the key being pressed. But unlike an email or word processor program, Cubase captures other data, such as how hard the note was played, how long the key was held, if it was pressed on while the key was down, and a myriad of other actions that can come from a MIDI Keyboard. For example, the sustain pedal being pressed, the pitch-bend and modulation wheels being adjusted, patch buttons being switched, and so on. Because MIDI can transmit and receive a great deal of nuance, the data stream of a MIDI Keyboard (or any MIDI controller) is much denser than a QWERTY computer keyboard.

## MIDI Is Actions

The creators of MIDI were some of the brightest minds in the music technology business. By designing the MIDI Specification, they provided musicians with a means to capture every action they could perform on a musical instrument. Notes are not the only actions that occur when a musician plays a musical instrument. For example, imagine a trombone player playing and sustaining a B. (Let's hope he can circular breathe.) After the note is played, there are a lot of things the player can do to accentuate the performance, such as adding vibrato, glissando, more volume, less volume, and growl. All of those nuances are added by performing some physical action on the instrument or by altering the way the air enters the horn.

# The Most Commonly Used MIDI Data

Now that you know that MIDI Data is comprised of actions, let's take a look at the most commonly used types of MIDI data.

## Notes

As we've discussed, pressing notes on your MIDI Keyboard will produce MIDI notes. Notes are depicted in MIDI by their note name and octave position as well as by MIDI note number. For example, middle C can be depicted as C3 (sometimes C4, depending on the brand of synth or software) and note number 60.

## Duration

As far as the MIDI Specification, there are note ons and note offs. The note offs determine when a note is released. However, musical notes are depicted by their duration. (Quarter-note, half-note, etc.) So even though the data that's being recorded when a note is released is being recorded as a note off, Cubase will represent this as duration.

## Velocity

The speed at which the key is being depressed equates to how hard the note is played. Velocity is a measurement of that speed. When a key is pressed slowly, it's played lightly like a *pianissimo*. When a key is pressed quickly, it's played hard like a *forte*.

## Aftertouch

While you're playing and holding a note, some synths and controllers record the pressure you apply to the key. This is known as aftertouch and usually adds vibrato or brightness to a sound, depending on what the synthesizer programmer had in mind.

However, I've seen a lot of newer MIDI controllers that are not aftertouch compatible. You'll need to read its owner's manual to find out if it can transmit aftertouch.

## Pitch Bend

Many synthesizers and MIDI controllers have one or two wheels on the left side of the chassis. One of them is the pitch bend wheel, which can simulate a trombone slide or a "whammy bar" on a guitar.

## Continuous Controllers

The MIDI Specification includes 128 separate MIDI control numbers. Some of those control numbers are dedicated, such as the sustain pedal (CC #4), modulation wheel (CC #1), and volume (CC #7). So if you're using any of those non-note controls to add nuance to your MIDI recording, they're being recorded as continuous controllers.

## Patch Select

These are the numbers assigned to the different sounds in your MIDI synth or sound-generating device. Early synths only came with thirty-two or sixty-four patches (a.k.a. sounds, instruments, programs, etc.), so the MIDI specification allowed for 128 patch select numbers. But as technology grew, so did the number of patches a synthesizer could hold. It's not uncommon to see thousands of patches in a modern synthesizer. So the MIDI Specification was modified to change two unassigned continuous controllers (CC #0 and CC #32, a.k.a. MSB [Most Significant Byte] and LSB [Least Significant Byte]) to Bank Select controllers.

## Beyond the Basics of MIDI

There is other MIDI data, such as system exclusive and MIDI clock. In an effort to keep MIDI accessible to you, I won't go over them in this book. If you do want to learn more about MIDI, I would recommend Hal Leonard's *The MIDI Companion Book*.

# When MIDI Becomes Sound

When all of the actions have been recorded on a MIDI track, there will come a time when a sound is generated. Another way to look at it would be the somewhat silly behavior of someone (not me, of course) playing "air guitar." The sound of the guitar will not be heard until you hand the mime a real guitar. (If the mime is playing air guitar inside an imaginary box, please maintain the illusion by first knocking on an imaginary door.) Then and only then will the sound be perceptible by others.

In the same way, you have to make a connection between the MIDI data (actions) and a device that can generate a sound. Early in my electronic music career, I made the mistake of assuming that MIDI was sound. I recorded a bass line on a MIDI track using my Sequential Circuits Prophet-5 synthesizer. When I played it back, I could hear the recording. Then I took my computer to a friend's house to have him listen to my musical idea. When I pressed play, no sound came out. I was baffled. I could see the MIDI data on the track, the time counter was running, and the cursor was streaming from left to right. Everything should have worked, except I didn't realize it was my Prophet-5 making the sound, not the computer. If I had brought along my synth and keyboard speaker, we'd have both been able to hear the sound. It is the instrument that generates the sound, not the MIDI data.

It also means that you'll need to have the audio outputs of each and every MIDI device plugged into some sort of mixer and/or speakers. Personally, I use multi-input audio interfaces (Steinberg MR816CSX) so that I can connect all of my MIDI synths simultaneously to my studio monitors. This is important, because you do eventually have to convert MIDI tracks to Audio tracks before you can mix your projects down to MP3 or audio CD. More on that later.

## The Invention of Multitimbral Synthesizers

Back in the 1980s, most synthesizers were monotimbral, meaning that they could only produce one sound at a time. Therefore, a composer needed an arsenal of synthesizers, samplers, sound modules, and drum machines to simultaneously generate the sounds for his or her MIDI tracks. For example, if I were working on a song that had five MIDI tracks, such as drums, piano, bass, saxophone, and marimba, I would have needed four synthesizers and one drum machine. Bear in mind that my prized Prophet-5 synthesizer could only play one sound at a time. I would have needed three more to hear all my MIDI tracks simultaneously. But at almost $4,000 each, I just couldn't afford more than one.

Then Sequential Circuits came out with a synthesizer called the SixTrak. It was one of the first multitimbral instruments on the market. As the term implies, a multitimbral synth can play back multiple sounds. In the case of the SixTrak, it provided me with simultaneous MIDI playback of up to six different sounds. In that configuration, each sound could only consist of one MIDI note. But since I was crafty, I used one note for the bass, one for the sax, four for the marimba; the piano notes (up to five) came from my Prophet-5; and the drums came from my Roland TR-505 drum machine.

Most of the synthesizers on the market since 1990 are multitimbral, so having only one synthesizer won't limit you to using only one sound or require a large investment in multiple synths. However, time and technology have introduced us to the wonderful world of virtual instruments. (Note: Virtual instruments can be either monotimbral or multitimbral.)

## The Invention of Virtual Instruments

The term *virtual instrument* can be a little deceiving. It's commonly misunderstood as the approximation of a real instrument (such as a piano or flute) coming from a synthesizer or sampler. What it actually describes is a synthesizer being generated inside of a computer. Earlier I told you that the computer doesn't make the sound of the MIDI track. However, with the invention of virtual instruments, you can use your computer as your recording studio and your synthesizers. In fact, today's modern computers can create virtual instruments that are more powerful and capable than a hardware or "real" synth.

In 1996, Steinberg created VST, or Virtual Studio Technology. With it came the capability of computers to generate hardware devices (such as signal processors and equalizers) in software. Later on, VST Instruments were added to the VST specification. VST Instruments are synthesizers and samplers created "virtually" in the computer. Virtual instruments are capable of generating very sophisticated sounds when played from a MIDI keyboard and can cost hundreds or thousands less than their hardware counterparts. But how is this possible? How can a computer generate such magnificent sounds?

The answer is easier than you might think. That's because digital hardware synthesizers are very similar to computers. They both have screens, a keyboard, CPUs, memory, storage, and an audio output. It's just that hardware synths are very specialized computers that don't surf the web, run accounting software, or send emails. While they do offer a wide range of musically useful functions, their primary purpose is to create sounds. By using virtual instruments, your computer can not only create sounds and record audio, but also run programs with which to surf the web and balance your budget. (Quick! Call Congress! Maybe they don't know about computers.)

# Cubase and VST Instruments

Cubase 6 comes with eight high-quality VST Instruments. While they all sound wonderful in their own right, we will be working with the most popular: HALion Sonic SE.

# Chapter 7

# RECORDING MIDI AND INSTRUMENT TRACKS

I was debating upon which recording chapter should come first: Audio or MIDI and Instrument tracks. I decided to follow my personal workflow. My musical endeavors always start with me sitting at my computer with Cubase and a MIDI Keyboard. Even if I'm planning to replace some of the MIDI tracks with "real" instruments, I record a lot of the early tracks as MIDI or Instruments. This allows me to listen to my ideas in context before I hire musicians or spend a lot of time creating Audio tracks that I may not use. It also allows me to map out the song form to see if all the sections flow together correctly. To that end, I'll start with MIDI and Instrument tracks.

However, I would strongly suggest that you read this chapter even if you plan to work with Audio tracks exclusively. I'm going to be introducing many of the Cubase recording fundamentals in this chapter. Therefore, it would behoove you to have a grasp of them. In this chapter, you will learn about:

- The relationship of MIDI and Instrument tracks.
- When to use MIDI tracks instead of Instrument tracks.
- Using the Browser with Instrument tracks.
- Recording your first Instrument tracks.
- The basics of editing MIDI data.
- Achieving the mouseless recording workflow.
- The concept of multitrack recording.
- Using the VST Instrument "rack."
- Using external sound devices with MIDI tracks.

## The Relationship of MIDI and Instrument Tracks

As I mentioned earlier, Instrument tracks are a combination of MIDI data that a virtual instrument converts to audio data. I sometimes say that Instrument tracks have a MIDI front end and an audio back end. You won't need to hook up and configure your MIDI synthesizers and/or sound modules. You'll just need to launch Cubase with your MIDI controller and audio interface connected to your computer. (You will, or course, need your studio monitors on or headphones plugged into your audio interface.) That makes it much easier for you to start learning about recording MIDI data.

## The Advantages of Instrument Tracks

Instrument tracks make it a lot easier to teach you about MIDI. Before the invention of virtual instruments, I'd have to make a lot of assumptions about what kind of synthesizers you owned and what sorts of sounds they could produce. With VST Instruments, you and I can be using the exact same sounds. So can the others you collaborate with either around town or around the world.

Another big advantage is the speed with which you can start recording. In a moment, you'll learn about the Browser (a.k.a. Sound Browser) and how to quickly audition and assign sounds to Instrument tracks.

While the cost advantage of virtual instruments is an important distinction, I find that the biggest advantage is how Cubase retains the instruments, tracks, sounds, and settings within the Project file. That means you can open your Cubase Project on any Cubase-equipped computer, and the project will sound identical to the computer upon which it was recorded (presuming that both computers have Cubase and the same virtual instruments installed upon them). Prior to virtual instruments, I'd have to make sure I had all the right sounds and all the right settings loaded into my hardware synths. If I didn't, the bass track might be playing a xylophone. Or the drum tracks might be playing piano sounds. While this made for instant avant-garde compositions, the results were usually less than predictable.

## The Advantages of MIDI Tracks

If you plan on using the sounds in your hardware instruments (such as your synthesizer, sampler, sound module, or drum machine), you'll need to use MIDI tracks. MIDI tracks can be assigned to the MIDI out port on your MIDI interface to transmit data to the MIDI input of external MIDI devices.

You can also use MIDI tracks with virtual instruments via the VST Instrument rack. This method gives you the advantages of virtual instruments. It also allows you to use multitimbral virtual instruments and route more virtual audio outputs to your Cubase mixer. That gives you the ability to mix and process the sounds more discretely.

# Recording Your First Instrument Track

Before we can proceed, let's create a new project using the empty template. (Review the procedure in "The Project Assistant," chapter 3.) When you name the Project Folder and the Project file, use the name "The Right Track X," where X is your name. On the DVD that accompanies this book, you will find a project named "The Right Track Matt," with several iterations of the examples I'll be using in the following chapters.

I should also mention that chances are slim that we'll be recording a Grammy winner. We're going to be making a lot of mistakes along the way, so don't turn into a perfectionist, at least not yet. The idea is to throw caution to the wind and get recording!

## Adding an Instrument Track

Add an Instrument track either by clicking on the Project menu, selecting Add Track, and then clicking Instrument; or by right-clicking in the Track column and selecting Add Instrument Track. The Add Instrument Track dialog box will appear and resemble either Figure 7.1 or Figure 7.2.

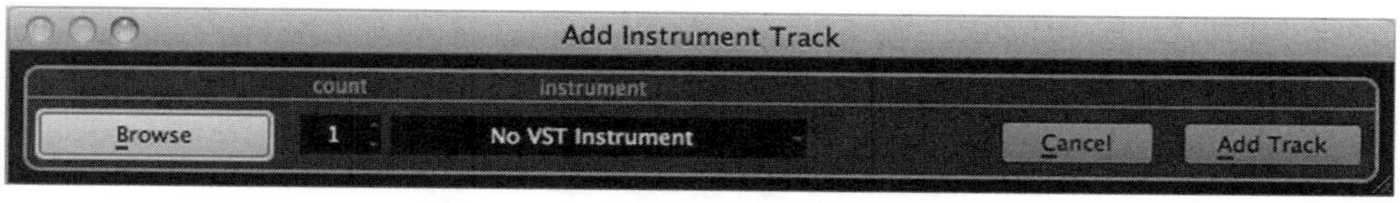

Figure 7.1: The Add Instrument Track dialog box with Browser closed

If your Add Instrument Track dialog box looks like the one in Figure 7.1, it means that your Browser is closed. Click on the Browse button to open the Browser.

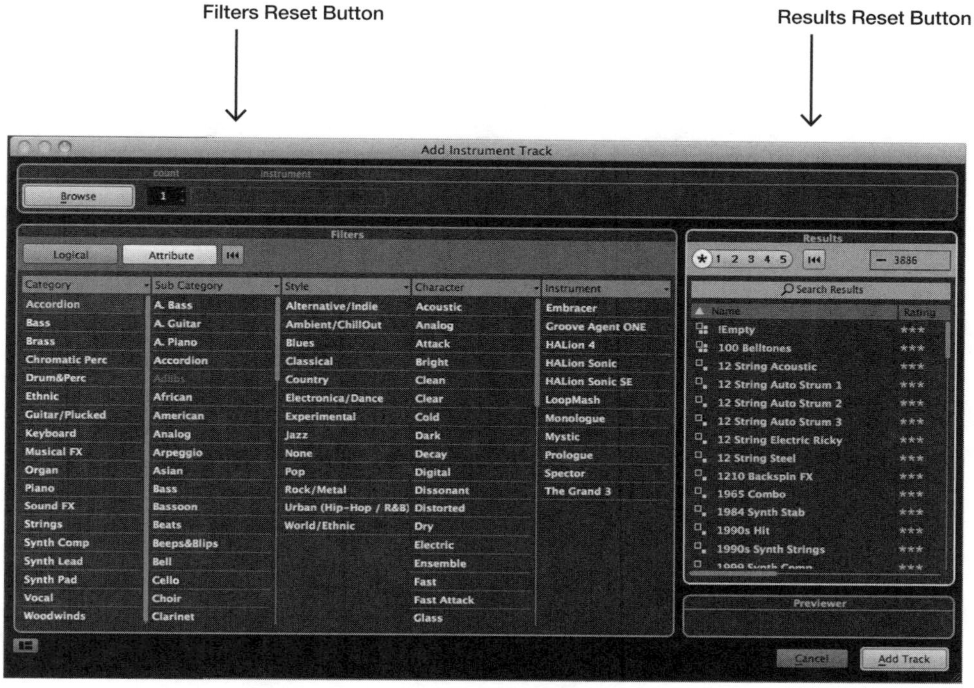

Figure 7.2: The Add Instrument Track dialog box with Browser open

Now your Add Instrument Track dialog box should look more like that in Figure 7.2. However, let's make sure that you and I are looking at the exact same thing. First, click on the Attribute button. Next, remove any previous selections by clicking on both the Filters reset and Results reset buttons. Finally, click on the Window Layout button and make sure that only the Filters and Previewer are checked, leaving the Location Tree unchecked.

## Auditioning and Choosing Sounds

Refer to Figure 7.2, and notice that the Browser is divided into a Filters section and a Results section. When in Attribute mode, the Filters section is subdivided into five columns, starting with Category and ending with Instrument. By making Filter selections, you can quickly narrow the Results column to the sounds you're looking for. The more columns in which you enable Filters, the narrower your Results will be.

Let's explore this concept further by clicking Piano in the Category column. Instantly the scope of the other columns becomes narrower. Now the Sub Category column displays Filters for A. Piano (Acoustic), E. Piano (Electric), and Other. Click on the A. Piano Sub Category. Now you can further refine your search by choosing a filter in the Style and Character columns. For now, leave those filters off. Instead, click on HALion

Sonic SE in the Instrument column. That way, the Results column will only display sounds that come from that VST Instrument.

With those filters enabled, the Results column will display a list of sounds that meet the criteria you chose in the Filters section. At the top of the Results section, you will see the sound named "[GM 001] Acoustic Grand Piano." Single-click on that sound, and a green highlight will appear on it, indicating its selection. After a short pause, the sound and its samples will be loaded, and you'll be able to audition it by playing your MIDI controller. Your Browser will appear as it does in Figure 7.3.

Figure 7.3: The Browser with Filters enabled

After auditioning the first sound, you may find it's not quite what you're looking for. You can single-click on other sounds in the Results column to explore other possibilities. On the right side of the Results column, you might miss the razor-thin scroll bar. Dragging the scroll bar will reveal more sounds. (If no scroll bar appears, then the Results column is displaying all the sounds that meet your Filter selections.) You can also hover your mouse pointer in the Results column and use your mouse wheel to scroll the list.

Once you've found the sound you want to use, you could click the Add Track button. However, let's choose something other than Piano. Click the Filter reset button. Then click on the Drum&Perc Category, then the Drumset Sub Category, then HALion Sonic SE in the Instrument column, and then scroll to the sound titled SR Alta Kit. Play some notes on the lower end of your MIDI keyboard to audition the sounds, and then click the Add Track button in the lower right-hand corner. The Add Instrument Track dialog box will disappear, and you will notice a new Instrument track added to your Track column. This track will have the same name as the sound you chose.

## Verifying Track Settings Prior to Recording

Before we press the Record button, let's take a look at our new Instrument track in Figure 7.4 and verify that all the settings are correct.

Figure 7.4: The new Instrument track

You will need to make sure that the track is record enabled and the MIDI Input and Output settings appear as they do in Figure 7.4. If you have a different section selected in the Inspector, make sure to click on the top section. Since the Add Instrument Track procedure set the Output to HALion Sonic SE, the only thing you'll need to do is verify that the Input is set to either All MIDI Inputs or the name of your MIDI controller that appears in the MIDI Port Setup of the Device Setup window. (See "Configuring Your MIDI Interface," chapter 3.)

## Filtering MIDI Aftertouch Data

Although it's not critical, I would recommend filtering MIDI aftertouch. If it gets recorded onto the Instrument track, it won't be a big deal. However, it will make it more difficult for you to see and interpret the MIDI data. The MIDI filters are located in the Preferences, which can be accessed from the File menu (Windows) or the Cubase menu (Mac). When the Preferences window appears, locate the MIDI Filter in the left column, then check the Aftertouch box in the right column.

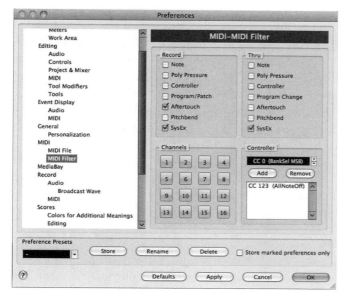

Figure 7.5: The Aftertouch MIDI Filter enabled

Click the Apply button, then the OK button, both of which are at the lower left-hand corner of the Preferences window. The Preferences are systemic, meaning that any changes you make affect Cubase globally. Therefore, aftertouch will be filtered during MIDI or Instrument track recording in every project from here on out. If you need to record aftertouch, repeat the procedure and disable (uncheck) the filter.

## The Logic Behind Starting with Drums

You may be asking why we're starting with drums. The reason is that when recording pop music, the drummer is usually the first musician to be recorded. This allows the drummer to provide the temporal grid upon which the other tracks will be recorded. After the drums are recorded, the other musicians will record their parts upon the foundation of the drum tracks. This makes for a very tight recording.

In the same way, even though I'm recording MIDI and Instrument tracks instead Audio tracks with a real drummer, I will create the foundation of the project with a virtual drum set. You can start with any instrument you'd like, but recording the drums first will make for a tighter recording.

## Drum Tracks Can Be Challenging

For nondrummers, creating a drum track can be tough. One of the best ways to learn what a drummer might play is to take some drum lessons from a drum teacher. That allows you to see and play the drums from a drummer's point of view. Armed with that knowledge and experience, you can record better virtual drum tracks in Cubase. Of all the money I ever spent on my recording studio, those drum lessons were probably the best investment I ever made.

To make it easier for you to get a drum track recorded, let's create arguably the simplest drumbeat found in pop music. Take a look at the drum notation in Figure 7.6.

Figure 7.6: The drum beat you will record

If you haven't recorded drums or read drum notation, let me talk you through it. Notice the lowest note on the staff. That's the bass drum, and you can find it on your MIDI controller by playing the second C below middle C. The next note up is the snare drum and is the second D below middle C on your MIDI controller. The highest note (represented with the X note head) is the hi-hat and is found on the second F♯ (F sharp) below middle C. (Those are MIDI notes C1, D1, and F♯1, and MIDI note numbers 36, 38, and 42, respectively.)

Now look at the counts beneath the notes. Notice that the bass drum notes land on 1 and 3, the snare drum notes land on 2 and 4, and the hi-hat notes land on 1 and 2 and 3 and 4 and. When you hear this beat played in its entirely, you'll probably say to yourself, "I've heard that drum beat before."

## Let's Record ... or Not

Now we're ready to record. However, if you'd rather not deal with drums right now, I've already recorded them for you. All you need to do is locate the folder named "The

Right Track" on the disc that came with this book and load the project named "The Right Track Matt R01 drums only.cpr." When the project loads, it will be activated. Your project will still be loaded but will become deactivated. Now single-click on the yellow event in the Event Display, and type Ctrl/Command + C to copy the event. Then type Ctrl/Command + W to close the "drums only" project, at which time your project will be reactivated. Type the "." key on your keypad to return the cursor to the beginning of the project. (You could also move the Left Locator to bar 1 and type the "1" key on your keypad to move the Cursor to the beginning of the project.) Verify that the Instrument track you added is still selected (see Figure 7.6), then type Ctrl/Command + V to paste the yellow event onto your Instrument track. You can then proceed to "Recording Your Second Instrument Track."

However, if you're the adventurous type, let's record the drum part. Verify that your Instrument track is record enabled (see Figure 7.6), and then click on the Transport menu and verify that Metronome On/Off and Precount On/Off are both checked. If they're not, click on them to activate them. If they're both unchecked, you'll need to go to the Transport menu twice. As a precaution, go to the Transport menu and click on Metronome Setup. Take note of the numeric value in the Precount Bars field.

Engage recording either by clicking the Record button on the Transport Panel or by typing the "*" (asterisk) on the keypad. You will hear the beeping of the Metronome during the Precount Bars, then the recording will engage. During the recording, you'll see an event being drawn in real-time on the Instrument track. You only need to record one bar of drums at this point. When you're finished recording, press the Stop button on the Transport Panel or type "0" on your keypad. To review your recording, press Play on the Transport Panel or type Enter on the keypad. If you're not happy with the recording, type Ctrl/Command + Z to undo the recording. Then repeat the recording process until you get a good take. (Note: We're going to be talking about the mouseless recording workflow in a moment; afterward, we will not be clicking on the Transport Panel buttons.) If you get the notes right, but the timing is a little (or a lot) off, don't worry about that right now. We'll deal with timing in a moment. For now, let's take a closer look at what we've recorded in Figure 7.7.

Figure 7.7: The MIDI event on the Instrument track (drums)

If you look closely at the MIDI event, you'll see some little specks through bar 1, after which they stop. Those specks are the MIDI notes you played. But you'll notice that the event continues on past bar 2. That's because it took you a moment to move your hands from the MIDI Keyboard and press the Stop button, during which time the recording proceeded.

# Basic Event Editing

Now that we've recorded an event, we can start learn the basics of editing, including resizing, repeating, and quantizing.

## Resizing the Event

Before going any further, we'll need to resize the event length so that it's precisely one bar long. Precision editing will require that Snap is enabled. (See "Cubasic #5: Snap," chapter 5.) Hover your mouse pointer over the event. Notice that when you do, you'll see small boxes in the lower corners of the event. These are known as handles.

### Cubasic #9: The Event Handles

The handles allow you to make different types of edits to an event, including repeating, which we'll learn about in a moment.

Figure 7.8: Event Handles revealed by hovering mouse pointer over event

But their most basic function is to allow you to increase or decrease the length or duration of an event. Move your mouse pointer over the right handle. You'll notice your pointer turns into a "left/right arrow" resize tool. Click and drag the handle very close to bar 2. (Snapping will resize the event precisely to bar 2.) When resizing the event, it will turn a much darker color. Don't worry, it just means the event is selected. When you release your mouse button, the event will appear as it does in Figure 7.9.

Figure 7.9: The event after it was resized

## Cubasic #10: Creating Repeats

Repeating an event is similar to a copy-and-paste command. But using the handles is a much more sophisticated method. Hover your mouse pointer over the right handle, at which time the pointer becomes a Resize tool. Now type and hold Alt/Option to turn the Resize tool into a Repeat tool, as seen in Figure 7.10.

Figure 7.10: The Repeat tool

The Repeat tool resembles a pencil. While holding Alt/Option, click and drag the right handle to the right. You will see the Repeat count appear to the right of the Repeat tool as it does in Figure 7.11.

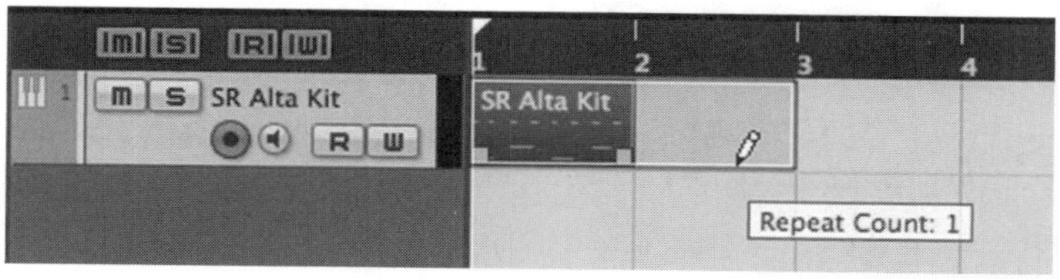

Figure 7.11: The Repeat tool and the Repeat count

The Repeat count will indicate how many times the event will repeat. The further to the right you drag the handle, the more repeats you will create. Go ahead and drag the event to create seven repeats so that it appears like Figure 7.12.

Figure 7.12: The result of repeating the event seven times

Now start playback from the beginning of the project. You'll hear that the original event repeats all the way through bar 8. This method is a great way to repeat events that occur over several bars. However, the Repeat tool can get overused. No musician can play the exact same performance over and over again. Every repetition would have differences in style, volume, timing, and other nuances that are not created by the Repeat tool. But since we're just getting started, we have a right to overuse these tools.

## Quantizing MIDI Data

Speaking of tools that get overused, let me introduce you to the concept of quantizing. *Quantizing* is a fancy term for quickly correcting your timing errors. In other words, when you play back a MIDI track and you hear some timing problems, quantizing the MIDI data can make the recording sound as though it was played much tighter. When MIDI recording programs first hit the market, they sort of auto-quantized the data. This was due to their low timing resolution. I remember using a pre-MIDI program that had 16 PPQ (pulses per quarter note) resolution. That meant that when I recorded a track, it would connect each note to the nearest sixteenth-note within the bar. The playback didn't sound like the freestyle performance that was recorded. Instead, it had the human groove stripped out of it and sounded more like a computer with perfect timing.

That's exactly what quantizing does: it makes the timing perfect. But perfect timing usually sounds boring. It certainly allows nondrummers to create much tighter-sounding MIDI drum tracks. But in stripping out the human timing element, "it-can-sound-ve-ry-mech-an-i-cal." For example, when you quantize a MIDI event to sixteenth-notes, the notes will be pushed or pulled to the nearest sixteenth-note. That's identical to that old program with 16 PPQ. When you consider that the timing resolution of Cubase is 480 PPQ, reducing it to 16 PPQ seems like a step backward.

### For Now, Let's Quantize

Now that I've told you that quantizing will strip the soul from your MIDI recordings, let's go ahead and do it anyway. Fortunately, Cubase gives us a number of quantizing methods, only one of which will result in a soulless mechanized feel. There's Quantize, Iterative Quantize, and Part to Groove. Each method will offer a different level of timing correction. Before we can quantize an event, it has to be selected.

### Selecting One Event

If you single-click on an event in the Event Display, it will become selected. Selected events are darker than unselected events on the same track. For example, single-click on the first event in your drum track, and it will look like Figure 7.13.

Figure 7.13: One event selected

If you were to perform a Quantize command now, it would only affect the selected event. However, since our drum track is made up of eight events, we'll need to select all eight of them.

### Selecting Multiple Events

There are a number of different ways to do this. Holding the Shift key and double-clicking the first event will select all of the events to the right. Typing and holding the Ctrl/Command key will allow you to select a series of contiguous or noncontiguous individual events. You can also type and hold the Shift key, and click and drag a selection box around the events, as in Figure 7.14.

Figure 7.14: A selection box

When you release the mouse button, all of the events between the start and end of the selection box will be selected. But if you want to select all of the events on a track, let me show you the fastest method. Right-click on the track (not the event) and choose Select All Events from the submenu in Figure 7.15.

Figure 7.15: The Select All Events command

You will notice that all of the events on the track will become selected. Now the Quantize command will affect all of the selected events.

### Setting a Quantize Value

The basic quantize settings are located on the left side of the Cubase tool bar.

The Quantize settings are divided into three sections. Clicking on the Quantize value in the center will open a list of Quantize values. For our drum event, a setting of 1/8 (eighth-notes) will be appropriate. So if it isn't set to the default of 1/8, click on it and choose that Quantize value.

### Performing the Quantize

Now go to the Edit menu and select Quantize or type "Q" on your computer keyboard. Then play the project to audition the Quantize results. Unless your timing was way, way off, the events will sound exactly like they look in Figure 7.6. The timing will be perfect, therefore sounding somewhat boring. Wouldn't it be nice if you could correct the timing with an adjustable level of perfection? Well you can, and it's called Iterative Quantize.

Figure 7.16: The Quantize settings

### Performing an Iterative Quantize

Type Ctrl/Command + Z to undo the first Quantize, then click on the Quantize/Iterative Quantize button (see Figure 7.16) so that it turns white and displays "iQ" instead of "Q." That will indicate that Iterative Quantize is enabled. Verify that all of the events are still selected, then repeat the Quantize procedure by selecting Quantize from the edit menu or typing "Q." When you play the results, you'll notice that some of the looseness of the original recording is retained, therefore making it sound more human than the first Quantize command. If it's still not as tight as you'd like it, repeat the Quantize command, and the Iterative Quantize will further tighten the timing. The default strength of the Iterative Quantize is 60 percent, which means that the notes are pushed or pulled within 60 percent of perfection. If you repeatedly use Iterative Quantize on an event(s), it will eventually become completely quantized.

### Undoing Any Quantize at Any Time

If the Quantize command was the last command you performed, you can type Ctrl/Command + Z to undo it. However, one of the magical things about Cubase is that you can undo the quantization anytime you'd like to, now or in the future. In other words, Cubase always retains the original recording and allows you to reset the quantization of any event(s). The event(s) you'd like to have returned to their original timing will first need to be selected. Then go to the Edit menu and select Reset Quantize.

# The Mouseless Recording Work Flow

When we recorded our first Instrument track, I provided you the option of using either the Transport Panel or keypad for transport control. However, I would strongly recommend that from now on, you use the keypad. You'll be using the Transport controls repeatedly throughout the recording process. By using the keypad and other key commands such as Ctrl/Command + Z for undo, you can dramatically increase the speed of your recording workflow. I call this the "mouseless recording workflow."

On the disc that accompanies this book, you will find a PDF folder that contains a file named "Keypad and Transport.pdf." It is a printable version of Figure 5.23 and shows the keypad and its associated Transport controls. Please print that PDF and place it where you can easily see it. It will help you learn this fantastically fast workflow. To that end, I will no longer be including the Transport Panel instructions during any recording process. You can still use the Transport Panel, but it will be much slower than using the keypad.

# The Concept of Multitrack Recording

Before we record our next Instrument track, it's a good time to talk about the concept of multitrack recording. Cubase, like all DAW software, allows you to record one track while you're listening to the previously recorded tracks. This is known as multitrack recording and remains one of the biggest revolutions in music production. But we have not always had the luxury of multitracking.

## A Brief History of Audio Recording

When audio recording became possible in the late nineteenth century, recording a musical performance meant that all the musicians had to play at the same time. Most ensemble groups didn't have a problem with this, because they always performed together in the same way. But it was also because the recording equipment of the era could only provide one track at a time. In the 1930s, magnetic (analog) tape recorders were invented. Recording suddenly became more accessible and affordable. The tape recorder also brought another revolution to market: stereo recording. In other words, some tape recorders had two tracks: one for the left and one for the right. Both tracks were recorded simultaneously and provided a much more realistic reproduction of sound.

Then in the early 1950s, a brilliant man named Les Paul (for whom the iconic Gibson Les Paul electric guitar is named) invented the process of ping-pong recording. Basically, he'd record his guitar onto a mono track on the tape recorder's left channel. Then he'd record the output of the left track into the input of the right track while he was playing a new guitar track. After the recording, the right track would contain the sound of the original track along with the new guitar track. He'd repeat the process back to the left track, which would then contain three guitar tracks. That left-to-right,

right-to-left procedure is how it got the name ping-pong recording. Using the ping-pong method, individuals could make ensemble-style recordings even if they were the only musician.

## The Invention of the Multitrack Recorder

In the '60s and '70s, the tape recorders became more than stereo recorders. By widening the tape and putting more magnets into the record/playback heads, track counts increased dramatically. The Beatles recorded on some of the earliest 4-track recorders. Before long there were 8-, 16-, and 24-track recorders, some of which could be linked together for even higher track counts.

Then in the early 1990s, Keith Barr of the company Alesis created the first affordable digital multitrack recorder, named the ADAT (Alesis Digital Audio Tape). Each ADAT had eight tracks that could be recorded onto an S-VHS tape. You could link up to sixteen ADATs together for a total of 128 digital tracks. Each ADAT cost about $4,000, so you did have to save your money to afford one, plus a mixer, outboard processors (such as compressors and reverbs), and a DAT (Digital Audio Tape) machine to mix down to. But if you really wanted to be on the bleeding edge, you could get a 1X CD burner for about $1,300. The blank audio CDs were around $60 each. (Making a toaster [a bad disc] back then was enough to ruin your whole day.)

## Cubase Has Spoiled Us Rotten

You are about to record your second track, thereby your first multitrack recording. Consider this: fifty years ago, what you're about to do could not be done at *any* price! The technology simply hadn't been invented yet. But now that you have Cubase, you can record unlimited MIDI, Instrument, and Audio tracks. The only limitations are the speeds of your computer and hard disks, and how much room you have left on your hard drive. All of the outboard processing can be done from within Cubase, and those processors are included in Cubase. Lest we forget that HALion Sonic SE had nine hundred built-in sounds you can add to your compositions, Cubase has provided us with an entire recording studio for less than $499. Sure we still have to buy the computer along with an audio interface, microphones, and other essentials. But the bottom line is that you have more power at your fingertips than the Beatles ever had when they were recording their iconic albums. Cubase really has spoiled us rotten. To that end, let's get back to recording.

# Recording Your Second Instrument Track

After the drummer packs up his drums, it's time for the bass player to lay down her tracks. In this case, we're going to repeat the Instrument track recording process, but this time we're going to record the bass guitar part. Therefore, we'll be repeating the recording process outlined in "Recording Your First Instrument Track" earlier in this chapter, except we'll need a different sound. When you get to the Browser as shown in Figure 7.17, click the Filter reset button. Then choose the Bass category, the E. Bass subcategory, the HALion Sonic SE instrument, and then the Dry Finger Bass sound. To create the Instrument track, click the Add Track button in the lower left-hand corner.

Figure 7.17: Choosing the bass sound for the Instrument track

You might have an idea of what you'd like to record for the bass track. Just in case you're feeling uninspired, Figure 7.18 will offer a suggestion.

Figure 7.18: A possibility for the bass track

Bass guitar parts are generally monophonic, meaning that only one note is played at a time. (Being a bass player myself, I know that's not always the case. But let's keep it simple.) Go ahead and record this example or your own inspiration on the new Instrument track, and remember to use the mouseless workflow.

## Using the Legato Function

When you have your bass line recorded, give it a listen. If it's anything like the bass line in Figure 7.18, it probably sounds choppy. Bass lines like my example are usually played legato, meaning that each note flows one to the other without any pauses in between. When a bass player plays legato notes on a real bass, the string continues to ring until the next note is played. But that's hard to recreate on a keyboard. So let's make the notes sound more like a real bass player is playing them by making the MIDI notes legato.

First, resize the event so that it is exactly eight bars long. Then make sure the event is selected, click the MIDI menu, go to Functions, and choose Legato. Now play the track, and you'll notice that the bass line is much smoother. The Legato function extends the end of every MIDI note to the beginning of the next note. It may not work every time, but when it does, it makes a huge improvement.

# Using MIDI Tracks with the VST Instrument Rack

You have seen how quickly your music can be recorded using MIDI data with Instrument tracks. However, using MIDI tracks along with VST Instruments loaded into the VST Instrument rack can provide you with options you don't get with Instrument tracks. The biggest advantages are accessing multitimbral VST Instruments and using more than one stereo audio output.

## Loading Instruments into the VST Instrument Rack

For this example, we're going to continue using HALion Sonic SE (which I will hereby refer to as HSSE). HSSE has both monotimbral and multitimbral operational modes. When you use an HSSE sound with an Instrument track, it's monotimbral. But when you install it into the VST Instrument rack and address it with MIDI tracks, HSSE becomes multitimbral.

You can access the VST Instrument rack by clicking the Devices menu or by typing F11 on your computer keyboard.

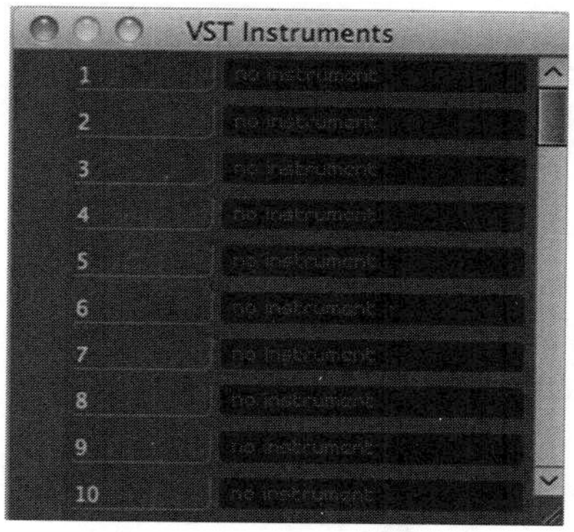

Figure 7.19: An empty VST Instrument rack

The VST Instrument rack is comprised of up to sixty-four numbered slots. In Figure 7.19, we can see ten empty slots. Click on the first slot where it says "no instrument" to reveal the VST Instrument list. (Note: The number and variety of VST Instruments that appear in the list may be more varied if you have installed third-party VST Instruments. Therefore, Figure 7.20 may contain instruments you do not have.)

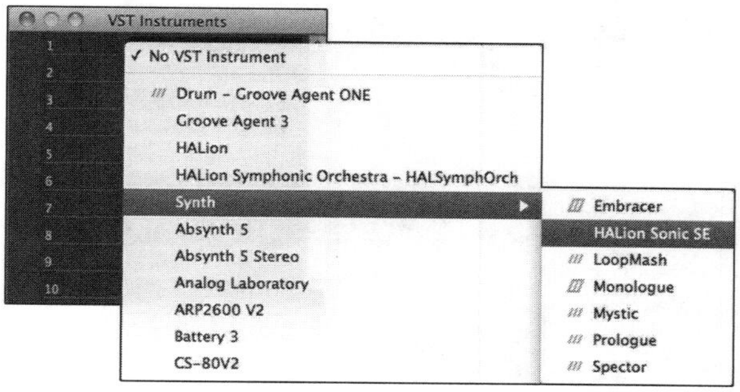

Figure 7.20: Choosing the HALion Sonic SE instrument

When the list appears, choose the Synth category, and then click on HALion Sonic SE. You will be prompted to add a MIDI track, so go ahead and click the Create button. A new MIDI track will be added to your project, and it will automatically be assigned to channel 1 of HSSE. You will also see the HSSE control panel.

Figure 7.21: The MIDI track and HALion Sonic SE control panel

## The HALion Sonic SE Control Panel

Think of the control panel as the front panel of a hardware synthesizer, which usually contains all the knobs and switches. On the left-hand side of the control panel, you will see sixteen numbered slots. These program slots are similar to the slots on the VST Instruments rack. However, instead of being used for VST Instruments, the program slots are where you load HSSE sounds, also known as programs. Let's take a closer look at those slots and some of the Inspector settings in Figure 7.22.

Figure 7.22: The Inspector and program slots of HALion Sonic SE

You'll notice that the MIDI track has been created for you, its MIDI Output is assigned to HSSE, and the MIDI Channel is set to 1. There are sixteen MIDI Channels just like there are sixteen slots on the HSSE control panel. Next to the channel number is the Edit Instrument button. Clicking this button will hide or reveal the control panel of the VST Instrument to which the MIDI (or Instrument) track is assigned.

### Loading Sounds (Programs) into HALion Sonic SE

This is another case of Cubase referring to "sounds" as programs, but the terms are synonymous. However, there is a significant difference between using VST Instruments and creating Instrument tracks: no specific sound selection takes place. There's a default sound called "First Contact" loaded into the first program slot, but HSSE chose that for you. Therefore, you'll need to add the programs you want to use.

In the far right of each program slot is a small triangle. That's the Load Program button. Clicking on it will open a Browser very similar to the one in Figure 7.17. The main item that's missing is the Instrument column, which makes sense, because you're looking at the HSSE control panel and therefore loading HSSE sounds/programs. Go ahead and load three different sounds into the first three slots of HSSE as I have done in Figure 7.22.

The MIDI track that was created for you should still be record enabled. That will allow you to audition the programs you're loading into the first slot. However, you won't be able to hear the sounds in any other slot. That's because the MIDI track is assigned to channel 1, therefore slot 1 of HSSE. To audition and record those programs, we'll need to create two more MIDI tracks.

### Adding More MIDI Tracks

Click on the Project menu, click Add Track and then MIDI, or right-click on the track column and select Add MIDI Track. The Add MIDI Track dialog box will appear, but if you see the Browser, click the Browse button in the upper left corner. Change the Count to 2, then click Add Track. You'll see two more MIDI tracks added to the Track column, and they'll have default names such as "MIDI 02" and "MIDI 03." You can, and I recommend that you do, change their names.

The next step is to change their MIDI Output and MIDI Channel settings in the Inspector. Click on the first new MIDI track, then change its MIDI Output to 1-HALion Sonic SE (at the top of the selection box) and its MIDI Channel to 2. Repeat the process for the second new MIDI track, but assign its MIDI Channel to 3. Now when you record enable the associated MIDI track and play notes on your MIDI controller, you'll hear the sounds you've assigned to the HSSE program slots 2 and 3.

In the "The Right Track" folder of the disc that accompanies this book, you can load the project "The Right Track Matt R01.cpr" to listen to the ideas I came up with in this chapter.

# Using MIDI Tracks with Hardware Synths and Devices

Up until this point, we've been totally ignoring any hardware synthesizers, sound modules, samplers, drum machines, or other MIDI-compatible devices you might have. But it's quite easy to add these devices into your Cubase Project as long as you follow two very important rules.

## Rule #1: Assign the MIDI Tracks to the Proper MIDI Output and Channel

The MIDI Output will need to be assigned to the MIDI Port to which the device is connected. For example, in Figure 7.23, I've created a new MIDI track and assigned it to Taurus-3 Bass Pedal. That's Moog Taurus-3 bass pedal synthesizer, which has its own built-in USB MIDI Interface (along with enough "bull power" to knock down walls). The setting you use will need to correspond to the MIDI interface to which your hardware device is connected. Bear in mind the device could have a built-in USB interface like my Taurus Pedals.

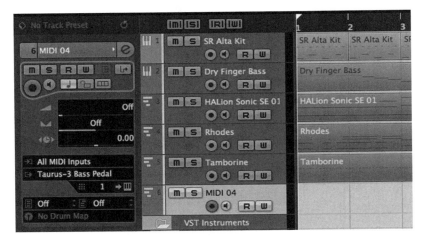

Figure 7.23: Inspector MIDI settings for an external device

The MIDI channel assignment will depend on the capabilities of your device. Some devices (like my Taurus pedals) are monotimbral and therefore only receive on one MIDI Channel. The device itself will have its own internal channel assignment, so the MIDI Channel setting for the MIDI track will need to equal that channel. However, if your device is multitimbral (like the Yamaha Motif), then you can create up to sixteen MIDI tracks and assign each to a different channel.

## Rule #2: The Device Audio Outputs Must Be Connected to Be Heard/Recorded

We know that MIDI is not sound. Therefore, making the proper settings in the Inspector is not enough to hear your external hardware device. The last step is to plug the audio outputs of each device into your sound system and/or audio interface. I use a multi-input audio interface (Steinberg MR816CSX) so that I can leave all of my external synths plugged in at all times. That also allows me to record an Audio track after I've recorded and edited the MIDI tracks. (That step is critical to incorporate the sound of your hardware synth[s] into the MP3 or audio CD mixdown file.)

To demonstrate this, let's assume you have one hardware synth you want to use in your Cubase Project. The synth audio outputs (the physical connectors on the device) need to be connected to something in order to be heard. If you're using a mixer, you could plug the device into that. However, I would recommend plugging the device directly into your audio interface, like I've done in Figure 7.24.

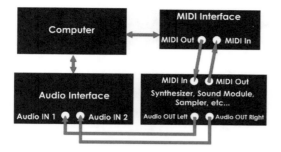

Figure 7.24: Recommended external synth wiring configuration

Now you need to create an Audio track and turn the Monitor button on. Also make sure to set the audio input to the physical input of the audio interface to which you've connected the external synth.

Figure 7.25: The new Audio track in monitor mode

Leaving the Audio track in monitor mode (Monitor button on) will allow you to hear the synth while you're recording the audio being generated by the MIDI tracks. Then when you're done recording and editing the MIDI data, you can record enable the Audio track and record the output of the synth onto that track. After the recording, you can disconnect the audio cables and power off the synth, because the Audio track will contain all the sound that it was generating previously.

# Testing 1, 2, 3, 4

There is a lot of music you can make with MIDI and Instrument tracks. But I'm guessing you'll be adding Audio tracks to your Cubase Projects. With that in mind, we'll be discussing Audio tracks in the next chapter.

# Chapter 8
# RECORDING AUDIO TRACKS

**M**any of the processes of recording Audio tracks are identical to those of recording MIDI and Instrument tracks. Therefore, it's a really good idea to read through chapter 7, because I cover many of those fundamental recording operations. This chapter will deal strictly with the fundamentals of audio recording, in which you will learn about:

- Choosing a monitoring strategy.
- Configuring Direct or Software monitoring.
- Setting proper input levels.
- The "line of sight" recording philosophy.
- Recording your first Audio track.

## Choosing a Monitoring Strategy

Before the invention of multitrack recording, there wasn't a need for sophisticated monitoring. Since all the musicians in the studio played at the same time, they just heard a monitor mix in their headphones. But with multitrack recording, each individual musician will record his or her tracks while listening to the prerecorded tracks. Therefore, he or she will need to hear a balance between the previous track(s) and the track(s) currently being recorded. That balance is critical for the musician to properly play against the tracks that had been recorded earlier. Too much of one and not enough of the other will result in a poorly performed recording. So how do we achieve a proper balance? There are two monitoring strategies with differing benefits. Basically, direct monitoring is when the performer hears the audio interface inputs and outputs simultaneously. Software monitoring is when he or she hears only the audio interface outputs. Let's take a closer look at these strategies.

## Direct Monitoring

This is by far the best choice for monitoring. The biggest advantage is that the performer will hear what he or she is playing precisely in time with the prerecorded tracks. This is known as zero-latency monitoring, wherein the performer monitors the inputs of the audio interface and the outputs of the prerecorded tracks simultaneously.

The disadvantage of direct monitoring is that it's harder to configure. The monitoring of Cubase is different with every audio interface. We'll learn about these differences in a moment. But there is another possible disadvantage: any processing added by Cubase (such as compression, EQ, and guitar amp effects) will not get recorded on the Audio track. With the exception of guitar amp effects (such as the VST Amp Rack), the disadvantage isn't as big as you might think, because any processing can be applied after the Audio track(s) has been recorded.

## Software Monitoring

Software monitoring allows the performer to hear his or her tracks along with any Cubase processing while listening to the prerecorded tracks. That processing will also become a permanent part of the recording. Software monitoring is also very easy to configure.

The biggest disadvantage is the latency performers will experience. Software monitoring requires Cubase to processes the audio before it can be sent to the output of the audio interface. Performers will notice a slight delay between when they play a note and when they hear it in their headphones. The severity of that delay (known as latency) will depend on the speed of the computer, sample frequency of the project, buffer size setting, and the number and type of processors being applied by Cubase.

## My Monitoring Advice

I would recommend configuring Cubase for direct monitoring and using the Tapemachine Style Auto Monitoring preference. (See "Auto Monitoring" below.) However, if you do want to record through plug-in effects (such as VST Amp Rack or the Vintage Compressor), you'll need to use software monitoring. We'll go over both strategies in a moment, but we'll also need to learn how to set up the Auto Monitoring in Cubase.

## Auto Monitoring

No matter which monitoring strategy you're using, you'll need to set the Cubase Auto Monitoring preference. Different settings will alter the functionality of the Monitor button on an Audio track. For Windows, click on the File menu and select Preferences. For Macs, type Command + , (the Command key plus the "," [comma] key) or click the Cubase menu and select Preferences. The Preferences window will appear as it does in Figure 8.1.

On the left side of the window, click on VST. Then locate the Auto Monitoring preference on the right. Click on the triangle to display the four Monitoring preferences.

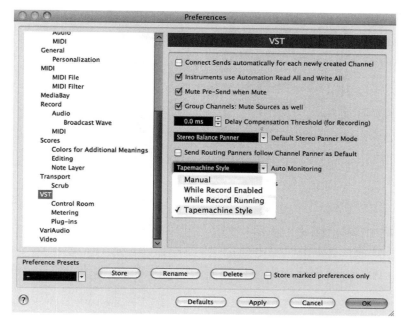

Figure 8.1: Auto Monitoring setting in the Preferences window

### Manual
The default setting is manual. This means that the Monitor button on the Audio track will need to be enabled and disabled manually.

### While Record Enabled
When you record enable an Audio track, the monitor will also be enabled. However, during playback, the monitor will need to be manually disabled so that the Audio track will be audible during playback.

### While Record Running
This enables the monitor only when recording is occurring. However, when recording has ceased, neither you nor the performer will be able to hear the input.

### Tapemachine Style
This is the setting I would recommend. It handles monitoring identically to that of an analog multitrack. When you record enable an Audio track, the monitor is also enabled. During recording, the monitor remains active. During playback, the monitor disengages, so that both engineer and performer can listen to the newly recorded track. When transport is stopped, the monitor reactivates.

## Disable Record on Selected Tracks Preferences
You may have noticed that when you select an Audio, MIDI, or Instrument track, the track automatically becomes record enabled. Up until this point, this has made the recording process easier. But now that we're going to use monitoring while recording Audio tracks, we need to disable the automatic record enabling. Otherwise, when you select an Audio track, the record enable and monitor will become active, and you won't hear the track play back. While you're still in the Preference window, locate Project & Locate both the Enable Record on Selected Audio Track and Enable Record on Selected MIDI Track (which includes Instrument tracks). They're both enabled by default. Uncheck each box, and then click the Apply button.

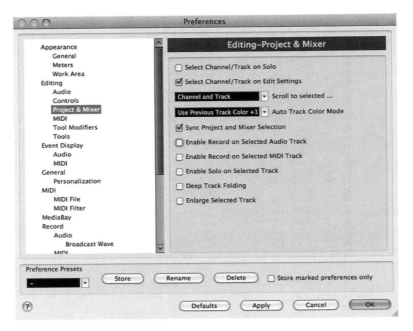

Figure 8.2: The Project & Mixer preferences

# Configuring Cubase for Direct Monitoring

As I mentioned previously, direct monitoring is more work to configure. However, both performer and engineer will enjoy its advantages. The most difficult part of describing the configuration will involve your choice of audio interface. Every manufacturer and model will employ direct monitoring in a different way. Therefore, I have to generalize the configuration of your audio interface.

## Enable Direct Monitoring in Cubase

Click on the Devices menu, and select Device Setup. From the Devices column on the left side, locate VST Audio System. Clicking on whatever appears below will display the driver options for your audio interface. In the case of Figure 8.3, it's my Yamaha Steinberg FW driver for the MR816CSX audio interface. With the driver options highlighted, enable the Direct Monitoring on the right side of the window, as it is in Figure 8.3.

You may need to hit the Reset and Apply buttons at the bottom of the Devices window to engage Direct Monitoring. You can then close the Devices window; however, we need to further configure your interface.

Figure 8.3: Direct Monitoring enabled on the driver options screen

## The Two Common Facilities for Direct Monitoring

This is where the configuration of Direct Monitoring gets difficult. Basically, your audio interface will have one or both of these facilities for configuring the all-important "input-to-output" balance.

### Mix or Balance Knob

Many of the sub-$500 interfaces have a mix or balance knob. The position of the knob will determine how much input versus how much output you're hearing. For example, the Steinberg CI series of interfaces have a mix knob, as shown in Figure 8.4.

Figure 8.4: The mix knob on a Steinberg CI2 audio interface

You'll notice that the extremes of the knob are labeled INPUT and DAW. Turning the knob toward INPUT will introduce more input signal and less playback signal. The opposite is achieved by turning the knob toward DAW. In other words, if you can't hear the performer you're recording (or the performer can't hear him- or herself), you'll turn the knob toward INPUT. If you (or the performer) is hearing too much of the performance you're recording, turn the knob toward DAW.

### Software-Based Monitor Applications (Programs)

Many of the more expensive audio interfaces (such as Apogee, Presonus, and RME) come with a monitor mixer application. That application is commonly installed during the driver installation process. Therefore, you probably already have it installed on your computer. You'll need to launch and configure the monitor application in order to take advantage of direct monitoring in Cubase. Consult either your audio interface owner's manual or the website of its manufacturer for more information.

However, to give you an idea of what I'm talking about, Figure 8.5 shows the TotalMix console that comes with certain RME audio interfaces.

Figure 8.5: The RME TotalMix monitor application

The best way to think of the monitor application is that it provides mixer functionality to your audio interface. Some of the sliders will control how much signal is coming from the hardware audio inputs, while other sliders control the playback output of Cubase to both you and the performer(s). By configuring the monitor application properly, you'll be able to achieve the requisite input-to-output balance.

## A Word About the Control Room

Cubase has a very sophisticated Control Room that allows you to customize all of your monitoring needs, including the creation of four separate headphone (studio) mixes. This allows you to feed different mixes to each performer of both prerecorded tracks and the tracks currently being recorded. For example, if the drummer needs more snare drum in his mix, you can increase the signal from that track without changing the balance in the three other headphone mixes. You can also assign the Click to any mix and adjust its volume. The Control Room is a very powerful tool for studio monitoring.

However, not everyone can take advantage of the Control Room for monitoring. First, your audio interface must have multiple outputs. That's not a tall requirement. But you must also have multiple headphone amplifiers and multiple headphones. The most important thing to realize is that you'll have to rely on software monitoring. That is, unless you have a Steinberg UR or MR-series audio interface such as the MR816CSX. Steinberg made it possible to use the UR and MR-series with all the features of the Control Room and still use direct monitoring. Other hardware manufacturers can add that functionality to their interfaces, but most of them still use a proprietary application to create monitor mixes. Personally, I love to have the Control Room and my MR handle the monitoring, because I don't have to switch between Cubase and another application.

# Configuring Cubase for Software Monitoring

Software monitoring is easier to configure than Direct Monitoring. However, there are some critical settings that will affect the monitoring operation and the latency it will induce.

### Disable Direct Monitoring

Refer to Figure 8.3 and disable Direct Monitoring. You may also need to hit Reset and Apply for the changes to take effect. Also, if your audio interface has a mix knob, turn it all the way to DAW, or totally opposite the inputs. If your interface came with a monitor application, make sure to turn down all of the input sliders.

### Setting the Lowest Possible Buffer Size

The round trip (input to output) the audio signal will make through your audio interface will introduce some latency—or the time it takes for the signal to enter the interface, be processed by Cubase, and then played back through the audio interface outputs. The audio interface buffer setting controls the amount of latency. Refer to Figure 8.3, and look at the Input and Output Latency. For my MR816CSX, the round trip will take about 5.5 ms (milliseconds) at the input, and about 5 ms at the output. That's a round-trip latency of about 11 ms. In an ideal world, the round trip would be 0 ms, but that is impossible with software monitoring. So it's imperative to reduce the latency as much as possible by lowering the buffer size. At the top of Figure 8.3, you'll find the Control Panel button. Clicking on that button will reveal a screen that will allow you to set the buffer size. If you're using Windows, the screen will vary depending on manufacturer. On a Mac, it will appear as it does in Figure 8.6.

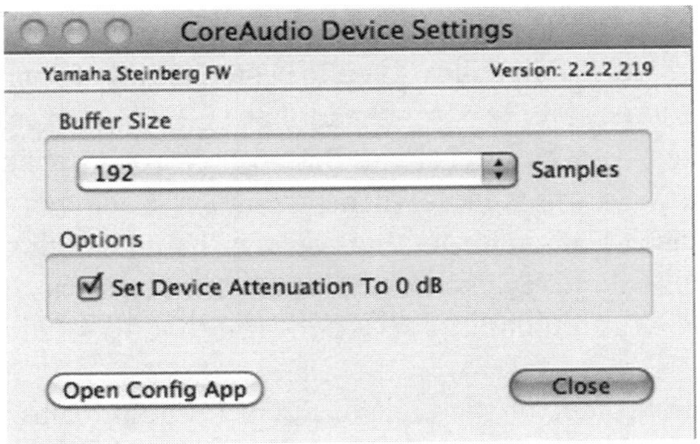

Figure 8.6: Control Panel with buffer size

The current setting of 192 samples will allow for the 11 ms round-trip latency. By lowering the buffer size to a value such as 128 or 64 samples, the latency times will be reduced. For example, if your project is set at 44.1 KHz, a setting of 64 samples would give you a round-trip latency of 4.5 ms. However, even if your driver allows for these extremely low buffer sizes, you may not get reliable performance.

### Keeping Your Latency Expectations Realistic

It takes a really fast, modern computer and a great audio interface with robust device drivers to achieve such low latencies. Even then, low buffer sizes can cause audible pops and clicks to appear in the audio signal. In some cases, the audio system may completely stop and require you to hit the Reset button on the Device Setup/driver options window. If you were recording at the time, the audio would contain anomalies and may not have recorded completely. Either way, the recording would be ruined. Therefore, low buffer-size performance should be thoroughly tested before recording any Audio tracks you want to keep. This limitation of software monitoring reveals the huge advantages of direct monitoring, wherein you can set very high buffer sizes and never hear the latency during the recording of Audio tracks.

However, the buffer size has a direct impact on the latency when recording Instrument tracks and VST Instruments with MIDI tracks. With all of this in mind, it's likely you'll be adjusting the buffer sizes several times while you're working on a project. It's a bit of a drag, but so is putting gas in your car and checking the tire pressure. Configuring latency is just something that has to be done when using any DAW software.

# Setting Up Your Audio Track

Now that we've made most of the preparations for audio recording, we can start making tracks. There will be a few more concepts I'll cover throughout the process. But at this point, make sure you have your "The Right Track X R01 Project" loaded. (See "Recording Your First Instrument Track," chapter 7.) Then go to the File menu, select Save As, and save a version of the project as "The Right Track X R02." (Remember, X = your first name.) This is so that you'll have a version of the project without the Audio tracks. That way, you can always revert to the earlier R01 version or any of its contents or settings.

## Adding an Audio Track

Adding an Audio track is similar to adding any track to Cubase: click on the Project menu, select Add Track, and then select Audio. You can also right-click in the Track column and select Add Audio Track. The Add Audio Track dialog box will appear as it does in Figure 8.7.

If the multicolumn Browser appears, click the Browse button. But before we add the track, we'll need to determine its configuration.

Figure 8.7: The Add Audio Track dialog box (Browser closed)

## Configuring the Audio Track

At the top of the Add Audio Track dialog box, you can choose how many tracks you want to add, the channel configuration, and what speakers the sound will come out of. The latter will be set automatically depending upon the mono or stereo configuration. (M = Mono, and L R = Stereo.) If your project was in a surround-sound configuration, you could choose which speakers to assign the track to. The count is set to 1 by default, but you could add several tracks at once if you so desired.

The configuration is the setting that takes the most consideration. In "When to Record in Mono, Stereo, or Multichannel" in chapter 4, we talked about counting your sources to determine whether a mono or stereo track was appropriate. In my case, I'm going to record my acoustic guitar using its built-in pickup. In other words, I'm going to take an instrument cable and connect the guitar's output to the audio interface input. That's one source, so I'll choose a mono configuration. However, if you're recording from more than one source (such as a stereo keyboard output or multiple mono sources), you'll need to choose a stereo configuration or add multiple mono tracks. When your configuration is set properly, click the Add Track button.

Figure 8.8: The new Audio track

In previous chapters, the new track would automatically be record and monitor enabled. Due to our changes in the Preferences window, they'll need to be enabled manually. But don't do it yet! If you do, you (and your ears) might be sorry.

### One Room + Microphone + Monitors = Headphones

If you are lucky enough to have a studio room (where your performer resides during recording) and a control room (where you and your computer are), you'll need to provide the performer with headphones and a monitor mix. However, most of us don't have separate rooms. Our microphone(s) and monitors are contained in one room. This presents a feedback problem. In other words, the sound from the microphone goes into the audio interface, then gets played out to the studio monitors, and then goes back into the microphone. This vicious cycle goes round and round, over and over again. The least it will do is color (in a very negative way) the sound of the recording and make it useless. The most it will do is cause uncontrollable squealing and howling to pour from your studio monitors. That will make the recording process impossible. Many try to control the feedback by turning down the studio monitors, but that will not solve the problem.

The only way to record with microphones in one room is to turn off (or completely turn down) the studio monitors and put on your headphones. If you are recording someone else, he or she will need to wear headphones too. In my case, even though I'm not using a mic, I prefer to wear headphones, because they'll provide a more intimate sound from my instrument. Plus, the disruption of air molecules (i.e., sound) emanating from the studio monitors can cause my guitar strings to vibrate and transfer the sound to the track. That's something I don't want to do. I want the Audio track to be recorded as purely as possible.

### The "Line of Sight" Method of Recording Signal Flow

Every audio engineer has his or her own philosophy regarding the signal flow getting to the audio interface. Some prefer to put signal processing (such as compressors, limiters, and equalizers) in between the source and input of the audio interface. That has the advantage of incorporating the processing directly onto the track. Others, like myself, prefer to leave the signal path as pure and simple as possible. In other words, connecting the source directly to the audio interface with one cable. I call this the "line of sight" method. This method presumes that any signal processing will be done after the track has been recorded. By using line of sight, you'll have plenty of options during the mixing process. You won't have those options if you incorporate the processing during the recording, meaning you'll have to get it right during the recording. Getting it right the first time can certainly be achieved but usually requires years of experience.

If you have an audio source that requires constant processing to achieve a characteristic, then line of sight won't work. But I would recommend that you keep the signal flow as simple as possible for another reason: noise. Every electronic device you add to the signal flow will add noise such as hum and hiss. That noise will get progressively more noticeable with every device you add to the signal path. The noise will become part of the recording, and if it's too noticeable or distracting, you'll need to rerecord the track(s) without the preprocessing.

### Setting an Appropriate Input Level

I almost added this as a Cubasic. But setting an appropriate audio input level is universal to the science of audio recording regardless of the device you're recording onto. The concept is to record with as much signal as possible without clipping (also known as peaking or distorting) the input of the audio interface. If you exceed the maximum input level of the audio interface, you'll be adding unwanted (and unflattering-sounding) distortion to the recording. Once it's there, you cannot remove the sound of clipping.

So why do we want to set a level as close to clipping as possible? The reason is to maximize the signal-to-noise ratio. The louder the signal, the less noticeable any noise will become. There's a control on every audio interface for setting the input level. Usually it's a knob or slider labeled "gain" or "level." In the case of my Steinberg CI2 (see Figure 8.9), it's called Gain, and each input has its own control. Along with that control is usually some sort of peak, clip, or OL (overload) indicator. My CI2 has red Peak indicators on each input channel, as shown in Figure 8.9.

Figure 8.9: The Gain knobs and Peak indicators on a Steinberg CI2

Setting the input level is actually a very simple process. The best way to do it is to sing or play the instrument as loudly as it will be played during the recording, and increase the gain knob (or equivalent) until the peak indicator (or equivalent) shows clipping. Then decrease the gain until the peak indicator no longer lights up. The rule is: you should never, ever, ever see the peak indicator during the actual recording. That's about it. (Note: I added a little "flash" indicator around the peak indicator on channel 1 to make it more visible.)

But with vocalists, they'll start to emote during the recording. When they do, they might sing more loudly than they did when you set the input level. Or in the case of instrumentalists, they might play more loudly or turn their own volume up without telling you. Either situation will result in an increase of input level that might cause clipping, thereby ruining the recording. Therefore, I always recommend setting the gain a little lower, just in case. Since your project is set to either 24- or 32-bit (see "Project Setup," chapter 5), you'll have a very wide dynamic range.

Some musical instruments will also have a volume control. For example, a synthesizer or keyboard will have a volume control, as will a pickup-equipped acoustic guitar or electronic drum set. If that's the case, make sure it's turned all the way up when setting the input level. That will further maximize the signal-to-noise ratio and also prevent the performer from manually increasing his or her volume beyond the point of clipping. (That's just one of a million tricks you'll pick up from working with volume-obsessed musicians.) However, if your gain control is turned all the way down and the input is still clipping, you might need to enable the PAD switch on the audio interface. If your audio interface doesn't have a PAD switch, decrease the volume control of the device you're recording.

# Recording Your First Audio Track

Now that you've added your Audio track, set its input channel and input level, and likely dawned your headphones and turned off your monitors, you can record and monitor enable the track. (See Figure 8.8.)

## Record on Measure 2, Not Measure 1

In Figure 8.10 (which is part of the "The Right Track Matt R02" on the disc that comes with this book), you'll notice that I've moved all of the events in the Event Display one measure to the right. I did this by performing a select all command (Ctrl/Command + A), then clicking on any event and dragging to the right. Then my recording starts at measure 1, but I didn't actually start recording until measure 2 … or did I? When you listen to the guitar track, you'll notice it plays before all the other tracks. That's because it has a few pick-up notes that occur inside of measure 1. If I had left the other events on measure 1 and started performing at that point, the recording would have missed those pick-up notes. But even if your performance doesn't include any pick-up notes, there's usually a few milliseconds of sound before the downbeat. If you miss them by recording too early, the track will sound chopped off at the beginning. For that reason, I recommend that you never place your Left Locator upon the measure where the performance begins. Always give yourself a measure to ensure that you capture the entire performance, including any pick-up notes or fleeting "human elements" that occur prior to the downbeat of the recording.

## Your Last Chance to Change Tempo

Up until this point, we've been using MIDI and Instrument tracks. That has allowed us the freedom to adjust the tempo (see "Project Tempo and Time Signature," chapter 5) at will. However, by recording an Audio track into this project, we have effectively set the tempo in stone. It's easy to change tempo with MIDI and Instrument tracks but much more difficult with Audio tracks. You'll usually end up with audible artifacts if you change the tempo of audio data, so it never sounds better than if you set the right tempo prior to recording. To that end, I've adjusted the tempo of "The Right Track Matt R02" from 120 BPM (beats per minute) to 112 BPM.

## Using Methods from Chapter 7

During the recording process, you'll be using many of the conventions you learned in chapter 7, including the mouseless recording workflow, the locators, and multitrack recording. Go ahead and do some recording, but remember that you're just practicing. If you take the recording too seriously at this point, the mistakes you'll be making might disillusion you. I really don't want that to be the case. I'd much rather you treat the recording process like that of learning a new musical instrument; you'll try, make mistakes, learn to avoid them next time, and the process will get faster and better each time. For example, take a look at Figure 8.10.

Figure 8.10: Matt is no "one-take wonder"

You'll notice I wasn't happy with my performance until take 08. While I'm embarrassed to admit it, that's an extraordinarily low number of takes for me. It's not uncommon for me to get into double, even triple, digits! I guess I practiced more when I was paying for studio time.

## Don't Let Me Stop You

From here, the world is truly your oyster. (Or if you're a vegetarian like me, the world is your tomato.) Using the MIDI, Instrument, and Audio track recording methods you've just learned about, you should keep recording. Remember that learning Cubase is exactly like learning a musical instrument. Therefore, you'll learn more when you practice every day. You'll also be making plenty of mistakes along the way. But it is learning from those mistakes that will move your education forward. I've provided you with some ideas to get started, but I'm guessing you have a lot of your own music to record. Get those ideas out of your head and into your Cubase Project with dispatch.

# APPENDIX: A GUIDE TO THE DVD-ROM

On the enclosed disc, you will find the Cubase Projects I used throughout the book and a PDF file. There are references to these files throughout the book, but let me explain a little bit more about them here.

## Files on the Disc

When you put the disc into your computer's optical drive and view its directory, you will see two folders: Cubase Projects and PDF. I would recommend copying both of those folders to your computer. They're not very large, so they won't take much space. While you could load and play the Cubase Projects from the disc, the slow speed of an optical drive will be a problem. Take a moment to copy both folders to a location on your computer where you can easily find them.

### Cubase Projects

Inside the Cubase Projects folder, you will find two Project folders: "My First Cubase Project" and "The Right Track." "My First Cubase Project" is used in chapter 4 for recording the test tracks, while "The Right Track" is used in chapters 5, 7, and 8. Loading the projects contained within each Project folder will allow you to see the features in Cubase that I was using while writing the book.

All of the MIDI or Instrument tracks are using HALion Sonic SE, which is one of the Cubase built-in virtual synthesizers. The Audio tracks were all recorded using a Steinberg MR816CSX. All Audio tracks were recorded direct without any additional processing between the instrument and the audio interface.

### "My First Cubase Project"

Inside this folder, you will find one Cubase Project titled "My First Cubase Project R01 .cpr." Double-clicking that Project file will launch Cubase (if it isn't already running) and load the project.

Figure A.1: Project window of "My First Cubase Project R01.cpr"

This is a very simple four-track project with data found on only three of the tracks. If you look at the Track column, you will see the following tracks: MIDI 01, Audio 01, Q-Stick, and Bass. MIDI 01 is assigned to the HALion Sonic SE VST Instrument and uses its default sound, First Contact. Audio 01 is an empty stereo Audio track. I added this so that I could tell you about the differences between stereo and mono tracks. Since I didn't record any stereo instruments, I added two mono tracks. Q-Stick was recorded with a RainSong WS-1000 acoustic guitar from its built-in pickup. Bass was recorded with a Status S2-Classic with EMG 40TW pickups.

## "The Right Track"

Inside this folder, you will find not one but three Cubase Projects that all share the same Project Folder. Using the project-revision-naming method I described at the end of chapter 3, "Using Matt's Project-Revision-Naming Method," you'll see that all three Project files have an RXX (e.g., R01, R02) added before the file extension. When you use this naming method, your own Project folders will start to look very much like "The Right Track."

### Project Window of "The Right Track Matt R01 drums only.cpr"

This project was created in "Recording Your First Audio Track" in chapter 7. It only has one Instrument track with the SR Alta drum set assigned to it. It has a one-bar drum pattern recorded at measure 1, and the Left and Right Locators are placed at measures 1 and 2.

Figure A.2: "The Right Track Matt R01 drums only.cpr"

As I describe in the book, you can start chapter 7 with this project if you'd rather not record drum parts. MIDI drum parts can be a challenge to record, and I'd rather you make progress quickly without getting bogged down. If you plan to use this project, load the Project file into Cubase, click on the File menu, and select Save As. Give it the name "The Right Track X R01.cpr" (X = your name). Then you can move on to "Basic Event Editing."

### Project Window of "The Right Track Matt R01.cpr"

This project contains all of the Instrument and MIDI tracks that were talked about by the end of chapter 7.

Figure A.3: "The Right Track Matt R01.cpr"

The first two tracks are Instrument tracks, while the last three are MIDI tracks, all of which use HALion Sonic SE for their sounds. The type of sound is included in each track name except for track 3, which displays the name of the VST Instrument (virtual synthesizer) to which it is assigned rather than the sound.

### "The Right Track Matt R02.cpr"

This is the project that was used throughout chapter 8. It is very similar to the "R01" version, except that all of the events on the MIDI and Instrument tracks have been shifted ahead one bar, and the Q-Stick Audio track contains a recording of a RainSong WS-1000 acoustic guitar from its built-in pickup.

Figure A.4: "The Right Track Matt R02.cpr"

The other major difference is that this version has been mixed a little bit. When I started recording the guitar, I noticed it getting lost in the other instrumentation. So I went to the Cubase Mixer and made some adjustments.

# Cubase Transport Controls on the Keypad

**From *The Power in Cubase:***
***Tracking Audio, MIDI, and Virtual Instruments***

**Matthew Loel T. Hepworth**

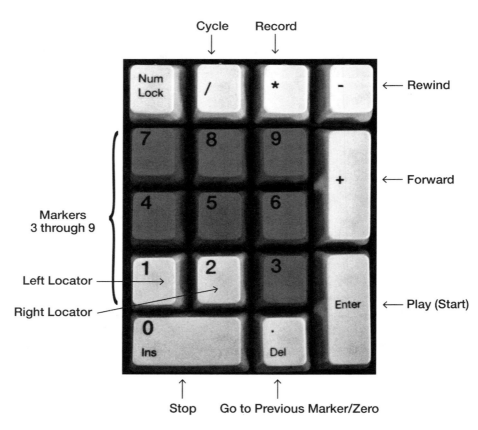

Figure A.5: "Keypad and Transport.pdf"

## PDF

Inside the PDF folder, you will find a file named "Keypad and Transport.pdf." This is a single printable page that shows where the Cubase Transport controls can be found on the numeric keypad. This is illustrated in "The Transport Panel" in Chapter 5, along with Figure 5.23.

I recommend that you print this PDF file and place it in a conveniently visible place in your studio. The sooner you learn to use these controls, the faster you can record your music with Cubase.

# INDEX

# quick PRO guides series

## Producing Music with Ableton Live
*by Jake Perrine*
Softcover w/DVD-ROM •
978-1-4584-0036-9 • $16.99

## Sound Design, Mixing, and Mastering with Ableton Live
*by Jake Perrine*
Softcover w/DVD-ROM •
978-1-4584-0037-6 • $16.99

## The Power in Reason
*by Andrew Eisele*
Softcover w/DVD-ROM •
978-1-4584-0228-8 • $16.99

## Sound Design and Mixing in Reason
*by Andrew Eisele*
Softcover w/DVD-ROM •
978-1-4584-0229-5 • $16.99

## Mixing and Mastering with Pro Tools
*by Glenn Lorbecki*
Softcover w/DVD-ROM •
978-1-4584-0033-8 •$16.99

## Tracking Instruments and Vocals with Pro Tools
*by Glenn Lorbecki*
Softcover w/DVD-ROM •
978-1-4584-0034-5 •$16.99

## The Power in Logic Pro: Songwriting, Composing, Remixing, and Making Beats
*by Dot Bustelo*
Softcover w/DVD-ROM •
78-1-4584-1419-9 • $16.99

## Logic Pro for Recording Engineers and Producers
*by Dot Bustelo*
Softcover w/DVD-ROM •
978-1-4584-1420-5 • $16.99

## The Power in Cubase: Tracking Audio, MIDI, and Virtual Instruments
*by Matthew Loel T. Hepworth*
Softcover w/DVD-ROM • 978-1-4584-1366-6 • $16.99

## Mixing and Mastering with Cubase
*by Matthew Loel T. Hepworth*
Softcover w/DVD-ROM • 978-1-4584-1367-3 • $16.99

*Prices, contents, and availability subject to change without notice.*

0312